Guatemalan Cookbook

Authentic Recipes

UNCOVER THE RICH AND DIVERSE FLAVORS OF GUATEMALA

SADIE E. RIVERA

GUATEMALAN COOKBOOK
Uncover the Rich and Diverse Flavors of Guatemala.

© Sadie E. Rivera
© E.G.P. Editorial

Printed in USA.
ISBN-13: 9798393358235

This cookbook is an exciting journey into the rich and diverse cuisine of Guatemala. It brings together a collection of traditional recipes passed down through generations, showcasing the country's unique blend of indigenous, Spanish, and Caribbean influences.

The recipes are simple and easy to follow, allowing you to recreate authentic dishes in your own kitchen. From appetizers to desserts, this cookbook covers a wide range of dishes that embody the bold and vibrant flavors of Guatemalan cuisine.

Whether you're an experienced cook or just starting out, this cookbook provides everything you need to bring the taste of Guatemala to your table.

Immerse yourself in the rich culture and history of this beautiful country and discover the delicious flavors that have been treasured for centuries.

Let's discover the wonders of Guatemalan cuisine!

TABLE OF CONTENTS

APPETIZERS

TOSTADAS

Ingredients:

- Corn Tortillas - 12
- Refried Beans - 2 cups
- Shredded Lettuce - 2 cups
- Shredded Cheese - 2 cups
- Sour Cream - 1 cup
- Salsa - 1 cup

Instructions:

1. Preheat oven to 375°F.

2. Place the corn tortillas on a baking sheet and bake for 8-10 minutes or until crispy.

3. Spread a layer of refried beans on each crispy tortilla.

4. Top each tostada with shredded lettuce, shredded cheese, a dollop of sour cream, and a spoonful of salsa.

5. Serve immediately and enjoy!

GUACAMOLE CHAPIN

Ingredients:

- Ripe Avocados - 4
- Tomatoes - 2
- Onion - 1
- Jalapeno Pepper - 1

- Fresh Cilantro - 1/4 cup
- Lime Juice - 2 tablespoons
- Salt - 1/2 teaspoon

Instructions:

1. In a large bowl, mash the ripe avocados with a fork or a potato masher.

2. Dice the tomatoes, onion, jalapeno pepper, and fresh cilantro, and add to the mashed avocado.

3. Stir in the lime juice and salt.

4. Taste and adjust seasoning as needed.

5. Serve with tortilla chips or use as a topping for tacos, tostadas, or any other dish.

CHILES RELLENOS

Ingredients:

- Poblano Peppers - 8
- Monterey Jack Cheese - 8 ounces
- Eggs - 4
- All-Purpose Flour - 1/2 cup
- Vegetable Oil - 1/2 cup
- Tomato Sauce - 1 cup

Instructions:

1. Roast the poblano peppers over an open flame or under the broiler until charred on all sides.

2. Place the roasted peppers in a plastic bag and let steam for 10 minutes to loosen the skins.

3. Peel the charred skin off the peppers and make a lengthwise slit to remove the seeds and membranes.

4. Stuff each pepper with 1 ounce of Monterey Jack cheese.

5. In a large bowl, beat the eggs until frothy. Add the flour and mix well.

6. Heat the vegetable oil in a large skillet over medium heat. Dip each stuffed pepper into the egg mixture and then place in the hot oil. Fry until golden brown on both sides, about 5-7 minutes.

7. Serve with tomato sauce on the side.

PLATANOS FRITOS

Ingredients:

- Ripe Plantains - 2
- Vegetable Oil - 1/2 cup
- Salt - 1/2 teaspoon

Instructions:

1. Peel the ripe plantains and slice them diagonally into 1/2-inch rounds.

2. Heat the vegetable oil in a large skillet over medium heat. Fry the plantain slices until golden brown on both sides, about 3-5 minutes per side.

3. Drain on paper towels and sprinkle with salt.

4. Serve as a side dish or as a snack with your favorite dipping sauce.

SALPICON

Ingredients:

- Cooked Shredded Beef - 2 pounds
- Tomatoes - 2
- Jalapeno Peppers - 2
- Red Onion - 1
- Fresh Cilantro - 1/4 cup
- Lime Juice - 2 tablespoons
- Salt - 1/2 teaspoon

Instructions:

1. In a large bowl, combine the cooked shredded beef, diced tomatoes, jalapeno peppers, red onion, and fresh cilantro.

2. Stir in the lime juice and salt.

3. Taste and adjust seasoning as needed.

4. Serve as a filling for tacos, burritos, or tostadas, or as a topping for nachos.

CHOJIN

Ingredients:

- Tomatoes - 4
- White Onion - 1
- Garlic Cloves - 2
- Jalapeno Peppers - 2
- Cumin - 1 teaspoon
- Fresh Cilantro - 1/4 cup
- Lime Juice - 2 tablespoons
- Salt - 1/2 teaspoon

Instructions:

1. In a blender or food processor, puree the tomatoes, white onion, garlic cloves, jalapeno peppers, cumin, and fresh cilantro until smooth.

2. Stir in the lime juice and salt.

3. Taste and adjust seasoning as needed.

4. Serve as a dipping sauce for tacos, tostadas, or as a marinade for meats and vegetables.

TORTITAS DE BERRO

Ingredients:

- Watercress - 2 bunches
- Potatoes - 2
- Eggs - 2
- All-Purpose Flour - 1/2 cup
- Baking Powder - 1 teaspoon
- Salt - 1/2 teaspoon
- Vegetable Oil - 1/2 cup

Instructions:

1. In a large saucepan, boil the watercress until tender. Drain and chop finely.

2. Boil the potatoes until tender. Drain and mash with a fork or a potato masher.

3. In a large bowl, beat the eggs. Add the mashed potatoes, chopped watercress, flour, baking powder, and salt. Mix well.

4. Heat the vegetable oil in a large skillet over medium heat. Scoop 1/4 cup of the batter into the hot oil for each tortita. Fry until golden brown on both sides, about 3-5 minutes per side.

5. Drain on paper towels and serve hot.

DOBLADAS

Ingredients:

- Corn Tortillas - 12
- Refried Beans - 2 cups
- Shredded Chicken - 2 cups
- Shredded Cheese - 2 cups
- Sour Cream - 1 cup
- Salsa - 1 cup
- Vegetable Oil - 1/2 cup

Instructions:

1. Spread a layer of refried beans on half of each corn tortilla.

2. Top the beans with shredded chicken and shredded cheese.

3. Fold the other half of the tortilla over the filling to form a half-moon shape. Secure with a toothpick if necessary.

4. Heat the vegetable oil in a large skillet over medium heat. Fry each doblada until crispy and golden brown on both sides, about 5-7 minutes per side.

5. Serve with a dollop of sour cream and a spoonful of salsa on the side.

6. Enjoy!

CHIRMOL

Ingredients:

- Tomatoes - 4
- White Onion - 1
- Garlic Cloves - 2
- Jalapeno Peppers - 2
- Apple Cider Vinegar - 2 tablespoons
- Fresh Cilantro - 1/4 cup
- Lime Juice - 2 tablespoons
- Salt - 1/2 teaspoon

Instructions:

1. In a blender or food processor, puree the tomatoes, white onion, garlic cloves, jalapeno peppers, apple cider vinegar, and fresh cilantro until smooth.

2. Stir in the lime juice and salt.

3. Taste and adjust seasoning as needed.

4. Serve as a topping for tacos, tostadas, or as a dipping sauce for meats and vegetables.

SALSITA DE CILANTRO

Ingredients:

- Fresh Cilantro - 1 bunch
- Tomatoes - 2
- White Onion - 1
- Jalapeno Peppers - 2
- Lime Juice - 2 tablespoons

- Salt - 1/2 teaspoon

Instructions:

1. In a blender or food processor, puree the fresh cilantro, tomatoes, white onion, jalapeno peppers, lime juice, and salt until smooth.

2. Taste and adjust seasoning as needed.

3. Serve as a dipping sauce for tacos, tostadas, or as a marinade for meats and vegetables.

CHICHARRONES

Ingredients:

- Pork Rinds - 2 pounds
- Salt - 1 teaspoon
- Ground Cumin - 1 teaspoon
- Chili Powder - 1 teaspoon
- Garlic Powder - 1 teaspoon

Instructions:

1. Preheat oven to 400°F.

2. Place the pork rinds on a baking sheet and bake for 15-20 minutes or until crispy.

3. In a small bowl, mix together the salt, ground cumin, chili powder, and garlic powder.

4. Sprinkle the spice mixture over the crispy pork rinds and toss to coat evenly.

5. Serve as a snack or as a topping for tacos, salads, and

soups.

ALBONDIGAS DE CHAYOTE

Ingredients:

- Ground Pork - 1 pound
- Chayote Squash - 2
- Garlic Cloves - 2
- Fresh Cilantro - 1/4 cup
- Egg - 1
- Salt - 1/2 teaspoon
- Vegetable Oil - 1/2 cup

Instructions:

1. In a large bowl, mix together the ground pork, grated chayote squash, minced garlic, chopped cilantro, egg, and salt until well combined.

2. Shape the mixture into 1 1/2-inch balls and set aside.

3. Heat the vegetable oil in a large skillet over medium heat. Fry the albondigas until browned on all sides, about 5-7 minutes.

4. Serve as a main dish or as a filling for tacos and burritos.

ELOTES LOCOS

Ingredients:

- Corn on the Cob - 4
- Mayonnaise - 1/2 cup
- Sour Cream - 1/2 cup
- Shredded Cheese - 1 cup

- Chili Powder - 1 teaspoon
- Lime Juice - 2 tablespoons
- Salt - 1/2 teaspoon

Instructions:

1. Preheat grill to medium-high heat.

2. Grill the corn on the cob until charred and tender, about 8-10 minutes, turning occasionally.

3. In a small bowl, mix together the mayonnaise, sour cream, shredded cheese, chili powder, lime juice, and salt.

4. Spread the mixture over the grilled corn on the cob, covering as much of the surface as possible.

5. Sprinkle with additional chili powder, if desired.

6. Serve immediately and enjoy!

GARNACHAS

Ingredients:

- Corn Tortillas - 12
- Refried Beans - 2 cups
- Shredded Cheese - 2 cups
- Lettuce - 2 cups
- Tomatoes - 2
- Sour Cream - 1 cup
- Salsa - 1 cup

Instructions:

1. Preheat oven to 375°F.

2. Place the corn tortillas on a baking sheet and spread a layer of refried beans on each tortilla.

3. Sprinkle shredded cheese on top of the beans.

4. Bake in the oven for 10-15 minutes or until the cheese is melted and the tortillas are crispy.

5. Top with shredded lettuce, diced tomatoes, a dollop of sour cream, and a spoonful of salsa.

6. Serve immediately and enjoy!

TAMALES DE ELOTE

Ingredients:

- Corn Masa - 2 cups
- Corn Kernels - 2 cups
- Shredded Cheese - 1 cup
- Baking Powder - 1 teaspoon
- Salt - 1/2 teaspoon
- Corn Husks - 12
- Vegetable Oil - 1/4 cup

Instructions:

1. Soak the corn husks in warm water for 30 minutes to soften.

2. In a large bowl, mix together the corn masa, corn kernels, shredded cheese, baking powder, and salt until well combined.

3. Spread a spoonful of the mixture onto each softened corn husk, leaving a 2-inch border at the top and bottom of the husk.

4. Roll the corn husk tightly around the filling, tucking in the sides as you roll. Secure with a piece of kitchen twine or a strip of the corn husk.

5. In a large saucepan, heat the vegetable oil over medium heat. Place the tamales in the saucepan and steam until cooked through, about 30-40 minutes.

6. Serve as a main dish or as a side dish with other traditional Guatemalan dishes.

SOUPS

PEPIAN

Ingredients:

- Chicken or Pork - 1 pound.
- Tomatoes - 3 medium sized.
- Garlic - 4 cloves.
- Onions - 2 medium sized.
- Coriander - 1/2 bunch.
- Cumin - 1 teaspoon.
- Black Pepper - 1 teaspoon.
- Pumpkin Seeds - 1/2 cup.
- Chiles - 2 medium sized.
- Vegetable Oil - 1/4 cup.

Instructions:

1. Heat the oil in a large pot over medium heat. Add the chopped onions, garlic, and chiles to the pot and cook until the onions are translucent.

2. Add the chopped chicken or pork to the pot and cook until browned on all sides.

3. Add the chopped tomatoes, coriander, cumin, black pepper, and pumpkin seeds to the pot and cook for 5 minutes.

4. Pour in enough water to cover the ingredients and bring to a boil. Reduce heat to low and let the soup simmer for 30 minutes.

5. Serve the pepian hot with tortillas or rice on the side.

CALDO DE RES

Ingredients:

- Beef - 1 pound.
- Potatoes - 2 medium sized.
- Carrots - 2 medium sized.
- Zucchini - 1 medium sized.
- Garlic - 4 cloves.
- Onions - 2 medium sized.
- Cilantro - 1/2 bunch.
- Cumin - 1 teaspoon.
- Black Pepper - 1 teaspoon.
- Lemon Juice - 1/4 cup.

Instructions:

1. In a large pot, add the chopped beef and enough water to cover. Bring to a boil and then reduce heat to low, let it simmer for 30 minutes.

2. Add the chopped onions, garlic, and cumin to the pot and cook for 5 minutes.

3. Add the chopped potatoes, carrots, and zucchini to the pot and cook for 10 minutes.

4. Stir in the cilantro and black pepper and let the soup simmer for an additional 10 minutes.

5. Stir in the lemon juice and serve the caldo de res hot with tortillas or rice on the side.

JOCON

Ingredients:

- Chicken - 1 pound.
- Tomatoes - 4 medium sized.
- Garlic - 4 cloves.
- Onions - 2 medium sized.
- Coriander - 1/2 bunch.
- Cumin - 1 teaspoon.
- Black Pepper - 1 teaspoon.
- Green Chiles - 2 medium sized.
- Tomatillos - 2 medium sized.
- Vegetable Oil - 1/4 cup.

Instructions:

1. Heat the oil in a large pot over medium heat. Add the chopped onions, garlic, and green chiles to the pot and cook until the onions are translucent.

2. Add the chopped chicken to the pot and cook until browned on all sides.

3. Add the chopped tomatoes, coriander, cumin, black pepper, and tomatillos to the pot and cook for 5 minutes.

4. Pour in enough water to cover the ingredients and bring to a boil. Reduce heat to low and let the soup simmer for 30 minutes.

5. Serve the jocon hot with tortillas or rice on the side.

CALDO DE GALLINA

Ingredients:

- Chicken - 1 pound.
- Potatoes - 2 medium sized.
- Carrots - 2 medium sized.
- Garlic - 4 cloves.
- Onions - 2 medium sized.
- Cilantro - 1/2 bunch.
- Cumin - 1 teaspoon.
- Black Pepper - 1 teaspoon.
- Lemon Juice - 1/4 cup.

Instructions:

1. In a large pot, add the chopped chicken and enough water to cover. Bring to a boil and then reduce heat to low, let it simmer for 30 minutes.

2. Add the chopped onions, garlic, and cumin to the pot and cook for 5 minutes.

3. Add the chopped potatoes and carrots to the pot and cook for 10 minutes.

4. Stir in the cilantro and black pepper and let the soup simmer for an additional 10 minutes.

5. Stir in the lemon juice and serve the caldo de gallina hot with tortillas or rice on the side.

SOPA DE ALBONDIGAS

Ingredients:

- Ground Beef - 1 pound.
- Bread Crumbs - 1 cup.
- Eggs - 2.
- Garlic - 4 cloves.
- Onions - 2 medium sized.
- Tomatoes - 4 medium sized.
- Coriander - 1/2 bunch.
- Cumin - 1 teaspoon.
- Black Pepper - 1 teaspoon.
- Vegetable Oil - 1/4 cup.

Instructions:

1. In a large bowl, mix together the ground beef, bread crumbs, eggs, and minced garlic until well combined.

2. Shape the mixture into small meatballs and set aside.

3. Heat the oil in a large pot over medium heat. Add the chopped onions to the pot and cook until translucent.

4. Add the chopped tomatoes, coriander, cumin, and black pepper to the pot and cook for 5 minutes.

5. Pour in enough water to cover the ingredients and bring to a boil. Reduce heat to low and let the soup simmer for 10 minutes.

6. Add the meatballs to the pot and let the soup simmer for an additional 20 minutes.

7. Serve the sopa de albondigas hot with crusty bread or tortillas on the side.

KAK'IK

Ingredients:

- Turkey - 1 pound.
- Tomatoes - 4 medium sized.
- Garlic - 4 cloves.
- Onions - 2 medium sized.
- Coriander - 1/2 bunch.
- Cumin - 1 teaspoon.
- Black Pepper - 1 teaspoon.
- Ancho Chiles - 2 medium sized.
- Vegetable Oil - 1/4 cup.

Instructions:

1. Heat the oil in a large pot over medium heat. Add the chopped onions, garlic, and ancho chiles to the pot and cook until the onions are translucent.

2. Add the chopped turkey to the pot and cook until browned on all sides.

3. Add the chopped tomatoes, coriander, cumin, and black pepper to the pot and cook for 5 minutes.

4. Pour in enough water to cover the ingredients and bring to a boil. Reduce heat to low and let the soup simmer for 30 minutes.

5. Serve the kak'ik hot with crusty bread or tortillas on the side.

SOPA DE FRIJOLES

Ingredients:

- Beans - 1 pound.
- Tomatoes - 4 medium sized.
- Garlic - 4 cloves.
- Onions - 2 medium sized.
- Coriander 1/2 bunch.
- Cumin - 1 teaspoon.
- Black Pepper - 1 teaspoon.
- Chiles - 2 medium sized.
- Vegetable Oil - 1/4 cup.

Instructions:

1. Soak the beans overnight in water or use canned beans for convenience.

2. Heat the oil in a large pot over medium heat. Add the chopped onions, garlic, and chiles to the pot and cook until the onions are translucent.

3. Add the soaked or canned beans to the pot and cook for 5 minutes.

4. Add the chopped tomatoes, coriander, cumin, and black pepper to the pot and cook for 5 minutes.

5. Pour in enough water to cover the ingredients and bring to a boil. Reduce heat to low and let the soup simmer for 30 minutes.

6. Serve the sopa de frijoles hot with crusty bread or tortillas on the side.

SOPA DE PATA

Ingredients:

- Pork Feet - 1 pound.
- Tomatoes - 4 medium sized.
- Garlic - 4 cloves.
- Onions - 2 medium sized.
- Coriander - 1/2 bunch.
- Cumin - 1 teaspoon.
- Black Pepper - 1 teaspoon.
- Chiles - 2 medium sized.
- Vegetable Oil - 1/4 cup.

Instructions:

1. In a large pot, add the pork feet and enough water to cover. Bring to a boil and then reduce heat to low, let it simmer for 30 minutes.

2. Heat the oil in a separate pan over medium heat. Add the chopped onions, garlic, and chiles to the pan and cook until the onions are translucent.

3. Add the chopped tomatoes, coriander, cumin, and black pepper to the pan and cook for 5 minutes.

4. Pour the contents of the pan into the pot with the pork feet and let the soup simmer for an additional 30 minutes.

5. Serve the sopa de pata hot with crusty bread or tortillas on the side.

SUBANIK

Ingredients:

- Pork - 1 pound.
- Potatoes - 2 medium sized.
- Carrots - 2 medium sized.
- Garlic - 4 cloves.
- Onions - 2 medium sized.
- Coriander - 1/2 bunch.
- Cumin - 1 teaspoon.
- Black Pepper - 1 teaspoon.
- Tomatillos - 2 medium sized.
- Vegetable Oil - 1/4 cup.

Instructions:

1. In a large pot, add the chopped pork and enough water to cover. Bring to a boil and then reduce heat to low, let it simmer for 30 minutes.

2. Add the chopped onions, garlic, and cumin to the pot and cook for 5 minutes.

3. Add the chopped potatoes, carrots, and tomatillos to the pot and cook for 10 minutes.

4. Stir in the coriander and black pepper and let the soup simmer for an additional 10 minutes.

5. Serve the subanik hot with crusty bread or tortillas on the side.

SOPA DE LIMA

Ingredients:

- Chicken - 1 pound.
- Limes - 4 medium sized.
- Garlic - 4 cloves.
- Onions - 2 medium sized.
- Coriander - 1/2 bunch.
- Cumin - 1 teaspoon.
- Black Pepper - 1 teaspoon.
- Green Chiles - 2 medium sized.
- Tomatillos - 2 medium sized.
- Vegetable Oil - 1/4 cup.

Instructions:

1. Heat the oil in a large pot over medium heat. Add the chopped onions, garlic, and green chiles to the pot and cook until the onions are translucent.

2. Add the chopped chicken to the pot and cook until browned on all sides.

3. Add the chopped tomatoes, coriander, cumin, black pepper, and tomatillos to the pot and cook for 5 minutes.

4. Pour in enough water to cover the ingredients and bring to a boil. Reduce heat to low and let the soup simmer for 30 minutes.

5. Squeeze the lime juice into the soup and let it simmer for an additional 5 minutes.

6. Serve the sopa de lima hot with tortillas or rice on the side.

SOPA DE POLLO

Ingredients:

- Chicken - 1 pound.
- Tomatoes - 4 medium sized.
- Garlic - 4 cloves.
- Onions - 2 medium sized.
- Coriander - 1/2 bunch.
- Cumin - 1 teaspoon.
- Black Pepper - 1 teaspoon.
- Green Chiles - 2 medium sized.
- Vegetable Oil - 1/4 cup.

Instructions:

1. Heat the oil in a large pot over medium heat. Add the chopped onions, garlic, and green chiles to the pot and cook until the onions are translucent.

2. Add the chopped chicken to the pot and cook until browned on all sides.

3. Add the chopped tomatoes, coriander, cumin, and black pepper to the pot and cook for 5 minutes.

4. Pour in enough water to cover the ingredients and bring to a boil. Reduce heat to low and let the soup simmer for 30 minutes.

5. Serve the sopa de pollo hot with tortillas or rice on the side.

SOPA DE CARACOL

Ingredients:

- Snails - 1 pound.
- Tomatoes - 4 medium sized.
- Garlic - 4 cloves.
- Onions - 2 medium sized.
- Coriander - 1/2 bunch.
- Cumin - 1 teaspoon.
- Black Pepper - 1 teaspoon.
- Green Chiles - 2 medium sized.
- Vegetable Oil - 1/4 cup.

Instructions:

1. Rinse the snails and let them soak in water for 30 minutes to remove any impurities.

2. Heat the oil in a large pot over medium heat. Add the chopped onions, garlic, and green chiles to the pot and cook until the onions are translucent.

3. Add the snails to the pot and cook for 5 minutes.

4. Add the chopped tomatoes, coriander, cumin, and black pepper to the pot and cook for 5 minutes.

5. Pour in enough water to cover the ingredients and bring to a boil. Reduce heat to low and let the soup simmer for 30 minutes.

6. Serve the sopa de caracol hot with crusty bread or tortillas on the side.

SOPA DE CHIPILIN

Ingredients:

- Chipilin - 1 bunch.
- Tomatoes - 4 medium sized.
- Garlic - 4 cloves.
- Onions - 2 medium sized.
- Coriander - 1/2 bunch.
- Cumin - 1 teaspoon.
- Black Pepper - 1 teaspoon.
- Green Chiles - 2 medium sized.
- Vegetable Oil - 1/4 cup.

Instructions:

1. Rinse the chipilin and chop into small pieces.

2. Heat the oil in a large pot over medium heat. Add the chopped onions, garlic, and green chiles to the pot and cook until the onions are translucent.

3. Add the chopped chipilin to the pot and cook for 5 minutes.

4. Add the chopped tomatoes, coriander, cumin, and black pepper to the pot and cook for 5 minutes.

5. Pour in enough water to cover the ingredients and bring to a boil. Reduce heat to low and let the soup simmer for 30 minutes.

6. Serve the sopa de chipilin hot with crusty bread or tortillas on the side.

SOPA DE CHAYOTE

Ingredients:

- Chayote - 2 medium sized.
- Tomatoes - 4 medium sized.
- Garlic - 4 cloves.
- Onions - 2 medium sized.
- Coriander - 1/2 bunch.
- Cumin - 1 teaspoon.
- Black Pepper - 1 teaspoon.
- Green Chiles - 2 medium sized.
- Vegetable Oil - 1/4 cup.

Instructions:

1. Rinse and chop the chayote into small pieces.

2. Heat the oil in a large pot over medium heat. Add the chopped onions, garlic, and green chiles to the pot and cook until the onions are translucent.

3. Add the chopped chayote to the pot and cook for 5 minutes.

4. Add the chopped tomatoes, coriander, cumin, and black pepper to the pot and cook for 5 minutes.

5. Pour in enough water to cover the ingredients and bring to a boil. Reduce heat to low and let the soup simmer for 30 minutes.

6. Serve the sopa de chayote hot with crusty bread or tortillas on the side.

SOPA DE PESCADO

Ingredients:

- Fish - 1 pound.
- Tomatoes - 4 medium sized.
- Garlic - 4 cloves.
- Onions - 2 medium sized.
- Coriander - 1/2 bunch.
- Cumin - 1 teaspoon.
- Black Pepper - 1 teaspoon.
- Green Chiles - 2 medium sized.
- Limes - 2 medium sized.
- Vegetable Oil - 1/4 cup.

Instructions:

1. Rinse the fish and chop into small pieces.

2. Heat the oil in a large pot over medium heat. Add the chopped onions, garlic, and green chiles to the pot and cook until the onions are translucent.

3. Add the chopped fish to the pot and cook for 5 minutes.

4. Add the chopped tomatoes, coriander, cumin, and black pepper to the pot and cook for 5 minutes.

5. Pour in enough water to cover the ingredients and bring to a boil. Reduce heat to low and let the soup simmer for 30 minutes.

6. Squeeze the lime juice into the soup and let it simmer for an additional 5 minutes. Serve the sopa de pescado hot with crusty bread or tortillas on the side.

SALADS

FIAMBRE

Ingredients:

- Carrots - 2, diced
- Beets - 2, diced
- Potatoes - 2, diced
- Green beans - 1 cup, chopped
- Peas - 1 cup
- Corn - 1 cup
- Cabbage - 1 head, chopped
- Mayonnaise - 1 cup
- Mustard - 2 tablespoons
- Onions - 2, diced
- Green olives - 1 cup, chopped
- Capers - 1/2 cup
- Lemon juice - 1/2 cup
- Salt - 1 teaspoon
- Pepper - 1/2 teaspoon

Instructions:

1. In a large bowl, mix together the carrots, beets, potatoes, green beans, peas, corn, and cabbage.

2. In a separate bowl, mix together the mayonnaise, mustard, onions, green olives, capers, lemon juice, salt, and pepper.

3. Add the mayonnaise mixture to the vegetables and mix well.

4. Cover the bowl and refrigerate for at least 2 hours or

overnight.

5. Serve cold as a side dish or as a main dish with bread or rice.

ENSALADA DE EJOTES

Ingredients:

- Green beans - 1 lb, cooked and drained
- Tomatoes - 2, diced
- Red onion - 1/2, diced
- Cilantro - 1/2 cup, chopped
- Lime juice - 2 tablespoons
- Salt - 1/2 teaspoon
- Pepper - 1/4 teaspoon
- Olive oil - 2 tablespoons

Instructions:

1. In a large bowl, mix together the green beans, tomatoes, red onion, and cilantro.

2. In a small bowl, mix together the lime juice, salt, pepper, and olive oil.

3. Pour the dressing over the vegetable mixture and mix well.

4. Cover the bowl and refrigerate for at least 30 minutes.

5. Serve cold as a side dish or as a main dish with bread or rice.

ENSALADA RUSA

Ingredients:

- Potatoes - 4, boiled and diced
- Carrots - 2, boiled and diced
- Peas - 1 cup, cooked
- Pickles - 1/2 cup, diced
- Mayonnaise - 1 cup
- Mustard - 2 tablespoons
- Onions - 1/2, diced
- Eggs - 4, boiled and diced
- Salt - 1/2 teaspoon
- Pepper - 1/4 teaspoon

Instructions:

1. In a large bowl, mix together the potatoes, carrots, peas, pickles, eggs, and onions.

2. In a separate bowl, mix together the mayonnaise, mustard, salt, and pepper.

3. Pour the dressing over the vegetable mixture and mix well.

4. Cover the bowl and refrigerate for at least 2 hours or overnight.

5. Serve cold as a side dish or as a main dish with bread or rice.

CURTIDO

Ingredients:

- Cabbage - 1 head, shredded

- Carrots - 2, grated
- Onions - 1, sliced
- Jalapeño pepper - 1, sliced
- Cilantro - 1/2 cup, chopped
- Lemon juice - 1/2 cup
- Apple cider vinegar - 1/2 cup
- Salt - 1 teaspoon
- Pepper - 1/2 teaspoon
- Sugar - 1 tablespoon

Instructions:

1. In a large bowl, mix together the cabbage, carrots, onions, jalapeño pepper, and cilantro.

2. In a small bowl, mix together the lemon juice, apple cider vinegar, salt, pepper, and sugar.

3. Pour the dressing over the vegetable mixture and mix well.

4. Cover the bowl and refrigerate for at least 2 hours or overnight.

5. Serve cold as a side dish or as a topping for tacos or burritos.

ENSALADA CHAPINA

Ingredients:

- Tomatoes - 2, diced
- Onions - 1/2, diced
- Cilantro - 1/2 cup, chopped
- Lime juice - 2 tablespoons
- Salt - 1/2 teaspoon
- Pepper - 1/4 teaspoon

- Avocado - 1, diced
- Cotija cheese - 1/2 cup, crumbled
- Tortilla chips - 1 cup, crushed

Instructions:

1. In a large bowl, mix together the tomatoes, onions, cilantro, lime juice, salt, and pepper.

2. Add the diced avocado and mix gently.

3. Sprinkle the crumbled Cotija cheese over the top of the salad.

4. Sprinkle the crushed tortilla chips over the cheese.

5. Serve immediately as a side dish or as a main dish with rice or beans.

PICADO DE RABANO

Ingredients:

- Radishes - 1 lb, sliced
- Tomatoes - 2, diced
- Onions - 1/2, diced
- Cilantro - 1/2 cup, chopped
- Lime juice - 2 tablespoons
- Salt - 1/2 teaspoon
- Pepper - 1/4 teaspoon

Instructions:

1. In a large bowl, mix together the radishes, tomatoes, onions, cilantro, lime juice, salt, and pepper.

2. Cover the bowl and refrigerate for at least 30 minutes.

3. Serve cold as a side dish or as a topping for tacos or burritos.

ENSALADA DE REMOLACHA

Ingredients:

- Beets - 2, boiled and diced
- Tomatoes - 2, diced
- Onions - 1/2, diced
- Cilantro - 1/2 cup, chopped
- Lime juice - 2 tablespoons
- Salt - 1/2 teaspoon
- Pepper - 1/4 teaspoon

Instructions:

1. In a large bowl, mix together the beets, tomatoes, onions, cilantro, lime juice, salt, and pepper.

2. Cover the bowl and refrigerate for at least 30 minutes.

3. Serve cold as a side dish or as a main dish with bread or rice.

ENSALADA DE CHAYOTE

Ingredients:

- Chayote - 2, peeled and diced
- Tomatoes 2, diced
- Onions - 1/2, diced
- Cilantro - 1/2 cup, chopped
- Lime juice - 2 tablespoons
- Salt - 1/2 teaspoon
- Pepper - 1/4 teaspoon

Instructions:

1. In a large bowl, mix together the chayote, tomatoes, onions, cilantro, lime juice, salt, and pepper.

2. Cover the bowl and refrigerate for at least 30 minutes.

3. Serve cold as a side dish or as a main dish with bread or rice.

ENSALADA DE GUISQUIL

Ingredients:

- Squash - 2, peeled and diced
- Tomatoes - 2, diced
- Onions - 1/2, diced
- Cilantro - 1/2 cup, chopped
- Lime juice - 2 tablespoons
- Salt - 1/2 teaspoon
- Pepper - 1/4 teaspoon

Instructions:

1. In a large bowl, mix together the squash, tomatoes, onions, cilantro, lime juice, salt, and pepper.

2. Cover the bowl and refrigerate for at least 30 minutes.

3. Serve cold as a side dish or as a main dish with bread or rice.

ENSALADA DE FRIJOLES

Ingredients:

- Black beans - 1 can, drained and rinsed

- Tomatoes - 2, diced
- Onions - 1/2, diced
- Cilantro - 1/2 cup, chopped
- Lime juice - 2 tablespoons
- Salt - 1/2 teaspoon
- Pepper - 1/4 teaspoon

Instructions:

1. In a large bowl, mix together the black beans, tomatoes, onions, cilantro, lime juice, salt, and pepper.

2. Cover the bowl and refrigerate for at least 30 minutes.

3. Serve cold as a side dish or as a main dish with rice or tortilla chips.

ENSALADA DE AGUACATE

Ingredients:

- Avocado - 2, diced
- Tomatoes - 2, diced
- Onions - 1/2, diced
- Cilantro - 1/2 cup, chopped
- Lime juice - 2 tablespoons
- Salt - 1/2 teaspoon
- Pepper - 1/4 teaspoon

Instructions:

1. In a large bowl, mix together the avocado, tomatoes, onions, cilantro, lime juice, salt, and pepper.

2. Cover the bowl and refrigerate for at least 30 minutes.

3. Serve cold as a side dish or as a main dish with rice or

tortilla chips.

ENSALADA DE NOPALITOS

Ingredients:

- Nopalitos - 1 can, drained and rinsed
- Tomatoes - 2, diced
- Onions - 1/2, diced
- Cilantro - 1/2 cup, chopped
- Lime juice - 2 tablespoons
- Salt - 1/2 teaspoon
- Pepper - 1/4 teaspoon

Instructions:

1. In a large bowl, mix together the nopalitos, tomatoes, onions, cilantro, lime juice, salt, and pepper.

2. Cover the bowl and refrigerate for at least 30 minutes.

3. Serve cold as a side dish or as a main dish with rice or tortilla chips.

ENSALADA DE PEPINO

Ingredients:

- Cucumbers - 2, sliced
- Tomatoes - 2, diced
- Onions - 1/2, diced
- Cilantro - 1/2 cup, chopped
- Lime juice - 2 tablespoons
- Salt - 1/2 teaspoon
- Pepper - 1/4 teaspoon

Instructions:

1. In a large bowl, mix together the cucumbers, tomatoes, onions, cilantro, lime juice, salt, and pepper.

2. Cover the bowl and refrigerate for at least 30 minutes.

3. Serve cold as a side dish or as a main dish with rice or tortilla chips.

ENSALADA DE ATUN

Ingredients:

- Tuna - 1 can, drained
- Tomatoes - 2, diced
- Onions - 1/2, diced
- Cilantro - 1/2 cup, chopped
- Lime juice - 2 tablespoons
- Salt - 1/2 teaspoon
- Pepper - 1/4 teaspoon

Instructions:

1. In a large bowl, mix together the tuna, tomatoes, onions, cilantro, lime juice, salt, and pepper.

2. Cover the bowl and refrigerate for at least 30 minutes.

3. Serve cold as a side dish or as a main dish with rice or tortilla chips.

ENSALADA DE ZANAHORIA

Ingredients:

- Carrots - 2, grated
- Tomatoes - 2, diced
- Onions - 1/2, diced

- Cilantro - 1/2 cup, chopped
- Lime juice - 2 tablespoons
- Salt - 1/2 teaspoon
- Pepper - 1/4 teaspoon

Instructions:

1. In a large bowl, mix together the grated carrots, tomatoes, onions, cilantro, lime juice, salt, and pepper.

2. Cover the bowl and refrigerate for at least 30 minutes.

3. Serve cold as a side dish or as a main dish with rice or tortilla chips.

VEGETABLES

GUISADO DE EJOTES

Ingredients:

- Green beans - 1 lb.
- Tomatoes - 2 large, chopped
- Onions - 1 medium, chopped
- Garlic - 3 cloves, minced
- Chicken broth - 1 cup
- Salt - 1 tsp.
- Pepper - 1 tsp.
- Cumin - 1 tsp.

Instructions:

1. Heat a large pan over medium heat and add the chopped onions and minced garlic. Cook until the onions are translucent.

2. Add the chopped tomatoes to the pan and cook until they are soft and mushy.

3. Add the green beans to the pan, followed by the chicken broth, salt, pepper, and cumin. Stir to combine.

4. Cover the pan and let the green beans cook for about 20-25 minutes or until they are tender.

5. Serve hot with rice or tortillas.

GUISADO DE CALABAZA

Ingredients:

- Squash - 2 lbs., peeled and chopped
- Tomatoes - 2 large, chopped
- Onions - 1 medium, chopped
- Garlic - 3 cloves, minced
- Chicken broth - 1 cup
- Salt - 1 tsp.
- Pepper - 1 tsp.
- Cumin - 1 tsp.

Instructions:

1. Heat a large pan over medium heat and add the chopped onions and minced garlic. Cook until the onions are translucent.

2. Add the chopped tomatoes to the pan and cook until they are soft and mushy.

3. Add the chopped squash to the pan, followed by the chicken broth, salt, pepper, and cumin. Stir to combine.

4. Cover the pan and let the squash cook for about 20-25 minutes or until it is tender.

5. Serve hot with rice or tortillas.

GUISADO DE GUISQUIL

Ingredients:

- Guisquil - 2 lbs., peeled and chopped
- Tomatoes - 2 large, chopped
- Onions - 1 medium, chopped

- Garlic - 3 cloves, minced
- Chicken broth - 1 cup
- Salt - 1 tsp.
- Pepper - 1 tsp.
- Cumin - 1 tsp.

Instructions:

1. Heat a large pan over medium heat and add the chopped onions and minced garlic. Cook until the onions are translucent.

2. Add the chopped tomatoes to the pan and cook until they are soft and mushy.

3. Add the chopped guisquil to the pan, followed by the chicken broth, salt, pepper, and cumin. Stir to combine.

4. Cover the pan and let the guisquil cook for about 20-25 minutes or until it is tender.

5. Serve hot with rice or tortillas.

GUISADO DE CHAYOTE

Ingredients:

- Chayote - 2 lbs., peeled and chopped
- Tomatoes - 2 large, chopped
- Onions - 1 medium, chopped
- Garlic - 3 cloves, minced
- Chicken broth - 1 cup
- Salt - 1 tsp.
- Pepper - 1 tsp.
- Cumin - 1 tsp.

Instructions:

1. Heat a large pan over medium heat and add the chopped onions and minced garlic. Cook until the onions are translucent.

2. Add the chopped tomatoes to the pan and cook until they are soft and mushy.

3. Add the chopped chayote to the pan, followed by the chicken broth, salt, pepper, and cumin. Stir to combine.

4. Cover the pan and let the chayote cook for about 20-25 minutes or until it is tender.

5. Serve hot with rice or tortillas.

GUISADO DE ZANAHORIA

Ingredients:

- Carrots - 2 lbs., peeled and chopped
- Tomatoes - 2 large, chopped
- Onions - 1 medium, chopped
- Garlic - 3 cloves, minced
- Chicken broth - 1 cup
- Salt - 1 tsp.
- Pepper - 1 tsp.
- Cumin - 1 tsp.

Instructions:

1. Heat a large pan over medium heat and add the chopped onions and minced garlic. Cook until the onions are translucent.

2. Add the chopped tomatoes to the pan and cook until they are soft and mushy.

3. Add the chopped carrots to the pan, followed by the chicken broth, salt, pepper, and cumin. Stir to combine.

4. Cover the pan and let the carrots cook for about 20-25 minutes or until they are tender.

5. Serve hot with rice or tortillas.

GUISADO DE PIMIENTO

Ingredients:

- Bell peppers - 2 lbs., chopped
- Tomatoes - 2 large, chopped
- Onions - 1 medium, chopped
- Garlic - 3 cloves, minced
- Chicken broth - 1 cup
- Salt - 1 tsp.
- Pepper - 1 tsp.
- Cumin - 1 tsp.

Instructions:

1. Heat a large pan over medium heat and add the chopped onions and minced garlic. Cook until the onions are translucent.

2. Add the chopped tomatoes to the pan and cook until they are soft and mushy.

3. Add the chopped bell peppers to the pan, followed by the chicken broth, salt, pepper, and cumin. Stir to combine.

4. Cover the pan and let the bell peppers cook for about 20-25 minutes or until they are tender.

5. Serve hot with rice or tortillas.

COLIFLOR RELLENA

Ingredients:

- Cauliflower - 1 large head
- Ground beef - 1 lb.
- Tomatoes - 2 large, chopped
- Onions - 1 medium, chopped
- Garlic - 3 cloves, minced
- Rice - 1 cup
- Salt - 1 tsp.
- Pepper - 1 tsp.
- Cumin - 1 tsp.

Instructions:

1. Cut the cauliflower into large florets and boil until they are tender.

2. In a separate pan, heat some oil over medium heat and add the chopped onions and minced garlic. Cook until the onions are translucent.

3. Add the ground beef to the pan and cook until browned.

4. Add the chopped tomatoes to the pan and cook until they are soft and mushy.

5. Add the cooked rice, salt, pepper, and cumin to the pan and stir to combine.

6. Fill each cauliflower floret with the beef and rice mixture and place in a baking dish.

7. Bake in the oven at 350°F for 20-25 minutes or until the filling is hot and the cauliflower is slightly golden on top.

8. Serve hot with a side of your choice.

GUISADO DE ESPINACA

Ingredients:

- Spinach - 2 lbs., chopped
- Tomatoes - 2 large, chopped
- Onions - 1 medium, chopped
- Garlic - 3 cloves, minced
- Chicken broth - 1 cup
- Salt - 1 tsp.
- Pepper - 1 tsp.
- Cumin - 1 tsp.

Instructions:

1. Heat a large pan over medium heat and add the chopped onions and minced garlic. Cook until the onions are translucent.

2. Add the chopped tomatoes to the pan and cook until they are soft and mushy.

3. Add the chopped spinach to the pan, followed by the chicken broth, salt, pepper, and cumin. Stir to combine.

4. Cover the pan and let the spinach cook for about 5-7 minutes or until it is wilted.

5. Serve hot with rice or tortillas.

GUISADO DE AYOTE

Ingredients:

- Ayote - 2 lbs., peeled and chopped
- Tomatoes - 2 large, chopped
- Onions - 1 medium, chopped
- Garlic - 3 cloves, minced
- Chicken broth - 1 cup
- Salt - 1 tsp.
- Pepper - 1 tsp.
- Cumin - 1 tsp.

Instructions:

1. Heat a large pan over medium heat and add the chopped onions and minced garlic. Cook until the onions are translucent.

2. Add the chopped tomatoes to the pan and cook until they are soft and mushy.

3. Add the chopped ayote to the pan, followed by the chicken broth, salt, pepper, and cumin. Stir to combine.

4. Cover the pan and let the ayote cook for about 20-25 minutes or until it is tender.

5. Serve hot with rice or tortillas.

FRIJOLES BLANCOS

Ingredients:

- White beans - 2 lbs., soaked overnight
- Onions - 1 medium, chopped
- Garlic - 3 cloves, minced

- Chicken broth - 1 cup
- Salt - 1 tsp.
- Pepper - 1 tsp.
- Cumin - 1 tsp.

Instructions:

1. Heat a large pot over medium heat and add the chopped onions and minced garlic. Cook until the onions are translucent.

2. Add the soaked white beans to the pot, followed by the chicken broth, salt, pepper, and cumin. Stir to combine.

3. Cover the pot and let the beans cook for about 1 hour or until they are tender and the broth has thickened.

4. Serve hot with rice or tortillas.

GUISADO DE CHILACAYOTE

Ingredients:

- Chilacayote - 2 lbs., peeled and chopped
- Tomatoes - 2 large, chopped
- Onions - 1 medium, chopped
- Garlic - 3 cloves, minced
- Chicken broth - 1 cup
- Salt - 1 tsp.
- Pepper - 1 tsp.
- Cumin - 1 tsp.

Instructions:

1. Heat a large pan over medium heat and add the chopped onions and minced garlic. Cook until the onions are translucent.

2. Add the chopped tomatoes to the pan and cook until they are soft and mushy.

3. Add the chopped chilacayote to the pan, followed by the chicken broth, salt, pepper, and cumin. Stir to combine.

4. Cover the pan and let the chilacayote cook for about 20-25 minutes or until it is tender.

5. Serve hot with rice or tortillas.

GUISADO DE NOPALITOS

Ingredients:

- Nopalitos - 2 lbs., chopped
- Tomatoes - 2 large, chopped
- Onions - 1 medium, chopped
- Garlic - 3 cloves, minced
- Chicken broth - 1 cup
- Salt - 1 tsp.
- Pepper - 1 tsp.
- Cumin - 1 tsp.

Instructions:

1. Heat a large pan over medium heat and add the chopped onions and minced garlic. Cook until the onions are translucent.

2. Add the chopped tomatoes to the pan and cook until they are soft and mushy.

3. Add the chopped nopalitos to the pan, followed by the chicken broth, salt, pepper, and cumin. Stir to combine.

4. Cover the pan and let the nopalitos cook for about 15-20 minutes or until they are tender.

5. Serve hot with rice or tortillas.

GUISADO DE BERENJENA

Ingredients:

- Eggplant - 2 lbs., chopped
- Tomatoes - 2 large, chopped
- Onions - 1 medium, chopped
- Garlic - 3 cloves, minced
- Chicken broth - 1 cup
- Salt - 1 tsp.
- Pepper - 1 tsp.
- Cumin - 1 tsp.

Instructions:

1. Heat a large pan over medium heat and add the chopped onions and minced garlic. Cook until the onions are translucent.

2. Add the chopped tomatoes to the pan and cook until they are soft and mushy.

3. Add the chopped eggplant to the pan, followed by the chicken broth, salt, pepper, and cumin. Stir to combine.

4. Cover the pan and let the eggplant cook for about 20-25 minutes or until it is tender.

5. Serve hot with rice or tortillas.

GUISADO DE YUCCA

Ingredients:

- Yucca - 2 lbs., peeled and chopped
- Tomatoes - 2 large, chopped
- Onions - 1 medium, chopped
- Garlic - 3 cloves, minced
- Chicken broth - 1 cup
- Salt - 1 tsp.
- Pepper - 1 tsp.
- Cumin - 1 tsp.

Instructions:

1. Heat a large pan over medium heat and add the chopped onions and minced garlic. Cook until the onions are translucent.

2. Add the chopped tomatoes to the pan and cook until they are soft and mushy.

3. Add the chopped yucca to the pan, followed by the chicken broth, salt, pepper, and cumin. Stir to combine.

4. Cover the pan and let the yucca cook for about 20-25 minutes or until it is tender.

5. Serve hot with rice or tortillas.

GUISADO DE COL

Ingredients:

- Cabbage - 2 lbs., chopped
- Tomatoes - 2 large, chopped
- Onions - 1 medium, chopped

- Garlic - 3 cloves, minced
- Chicken broth - 1 cup
- Salt - 1 tsp.
- Pepper - 1 tsp.
- Cumin - 1 tsp.

Instructions:

1. Heat a large pan over medium heat and add the chopped onions and minced garlic. Cook until the onions are translucent.

2. Add the chopped tomatoes to the pan and cook until they are soft and mushy.

3. Add the chopped cabbage to the pan, followed by the chicken broth, salt, pepper, and cumin. Stir to combine.

4. Cover the pan and let the cabbage cook for about 15-20 minutes or until it is tender.

5. Serve hot with rice or tortillas.

SIDE DISHES

ARROZ CHAPIN

Ingredients:

- Rice - 2 cups
- Water - 4 cups
- Saffron - a pinch
- Garlic - 2 cloves
- Onion - 1 chopped
- Tomatoes - 2 chopped
- Salt - to taste

Instructions:

1. Rinse the rice and place it in a pot with 4 cups of water.

2. Add the saffron, salt, and garlic to the pot and bring it to a boil.

3. Reduce the heat to low and let it simmer for about 20 minutes.

4. In a separate pan, saute the chopped onion and tomatoes until softened.

5. Add the sauteed mixture to the pot with the rice and stir well.

6. Continue to let it simmer for another 10 minutes or until the rice is fully cooked.

TAMALITOS DE CHIPILIN

Ingredients:

- Maize Flour - 2 cups
- Water - 4 cups
- Chipilin - 1 cup chopped
- Tomatoes - 2 chopped
- Onion - 1 chopped
- Garlic - 2 cloves
- Salt - to taste

Instructions:

1. In a pot, bring the 4 cups of water to a boil.

2. Add the maize flour to the boiling water and stir until it forms a dough-like consistency.

3. In a separate pan, saute the chopped onion, tomatoes, garlic, and chipilin until softened.

4. Add the sauteed mixture to the maize dough and mix well.

5. Divide the dough into small portions and wrap them in banana leaves or foil.

6. Place the wrapped tamalitos in a steamer and let them steam for about 20-30 minutes.

RELLENITOS

Ingredients:

- Black Beans - 2 cups
- Masarina Flour - 2 cups

- Water - 1 cup
- Cinnamon - 1 tsp
- Sugar - 1/2 cup
- Vegetable Oil - for frying

Instructions:

1. In a pot, cook the black beans until soft and mash them into a paste.

2. In a separate bowl, mix the masarina flour, water, cinnamon, and sugar to form a dough.

3. Divide the dough into small portions and flatten them into circles.

4. Place a spoonful of the mashed black beans in the center of each dough circle.

5. Fold the edges of the dough over the black beans to form a pocket and seal it closed.

6. Heat the vegetable oil in a pan and fry the rellenos until they are golden brown on both sides.

PACAYAS ENVUELTAS

Ingredients:

- Pacayas - 4 whole
- Corn Husks - 8
- Water - 1 cup
- Salt - to taste

Instructions:

1. Clean and remove the thorns from the pacayas.

2. Soak the corn husks in water for about 10 minutes to soften them.

3. Place one pacaya in the center of each corn husk and sprinkle with salt.

4. Fold the sides of the corn husks over the pacaya and wrap them tightly.

5. Place the wrapped pacayas in a pot and add 1 cup of water.

6. Bring the water to a boil, then reduce the heat to low and let the pacayas steam for about 20-30 minutes.

FRIJOLES PARADOS

Ingredients:

- Black Beans - 2 cups
- Water - 4 cups
- Garlic - 2 cloves
- Onion - 1 chopped
- Tomatoes - 2 chopped
- Cilantro - 1/2 cup chopped
- Salt - to taste

Instructions:

1. Rinse the black beans and place them in a pot with 4 cups of water.

2. Add the garlic and salt to the pot and bring it to a boil.

3. Reduce the heat to low and let the beans simmer for about 30 minutes or until they are soft.

4. In a separate pan, saute the chopped onion and tomatoes until softened.

5. Drain the cooked beans and add the sauteed mixture to the pot with the beans.

6. Mash the beans with a fork or potato masher until they form a rough paste.

7. Stir in the chopped cilantro and serve the frijoles parados hot.

YUCA CON CHICHARRON

Ingredients:

- Yuca - 4 large
- Water - 8 cups
- Salt - to taste
- Chicharron - 1 pound
- Garlic - 2 cloves
- Onion - 1 chopped
- Lime - 1 cut into wedges

Instructions:

1. Peel and chop the yuca into large pieces.

2. Place the yuca in a pot with 8 cups of water and a pinch of salt.

3. Bring the water to a boil, then reduce the heat to low and let the yuca simmer for about 20-25 minutes or until it is tender.

4. Drain the yuca and set it aside.

5. In a separate pan, saute the chopped onion and garlic until softened.

6. Add the chicharron to the pan and continue to cook until crispy.

7. Serve the yuca hot, topped with the chicharron mixture and a squeeze of lime juice.

ARROZ CON VEGETALES

Ingredients:

- Rice - 2 cups
- Water - 4 cups
- Carrots - 1 chopped
- Zucchini - 1 chopped
- Peas - 1 cup
- Garlic - 2 cloves
- Onion - 1 chopped
- Salt - to taste

Instructions:

1. Rinse the rice and place it in a pot with 4 cups of water.

2. Add the garlic, salt, and onion to the pot and bring it to a boil.

3. Reduce the heat to low and let the rice simmer for about 20 minutes.

4. In a separate pan, saute the chopped carrots, zucchini, and peas until softened.

5. Add the sauteed vegetables to the pot with the rice and

stir well.

6. Continue to let the rice simmer for another 10 minutes or until it is fully cooked and all the liquid has been absorbed.

PATACONES

Ingredients:

- Green Plantains - 4
- Vegetable Oil - for frying
- Salt - to taste

Instructions:

1. Peel the green plantains and slice them into rounds about 1/2 inch thick.

2. Heat the vegetable oil in a pan over medium heat.

3. Fry the plantain rounds until they are golden brown on both sides, about 2-3 minutes per side.

4. Remove the plantains from the oil and place them on a paper towel to drain any excess oil.

5. Use a flat surface such as a plate or cutting board to press down on the plantains to flatten them into rounds about 1/4 inch thick.

6. Re-fry the flattened plantains until they are crispy and golden brown on both sides, about 2-3 minutes per side.

7. Sprinkle salt over the patacones and serve hot as a side dish.

FRIJOLES VOLTEADOS

Ingredients:

- Black Beans - 2 cups
- Water - 4 cups
- Rice - 2 cups
- Garlic - 2 cloves
- Tomatoes - 2 chopped
- Onion - 1 chopped
- Cilantro - 1/2 cup chopped
- Salt - to taste

Instructions:

1. Rinse the black beans and place them in a pot with 4 cups of water.

2. Add the garlic and salt to the pot and bring it to a boil.

3. Reduce the heat to low and let the beans simmer for about 30 minutes or until they are soft.

4. In a separate pan, saute the chopped onion, tomatoes, and cilantro until softened.

5. Drain the cooked beans and add the sauteed mixture to the pot with the beans.

6. Mash the beans with a fork or potato masher until they form a rough paste.

7. Cook the rice according to package instructions.

8. Spread the mashed beans on a large serving platter and top with the cooked rice.

9. Use a spatula to turn the rice and beans over so that the rice is on the bottom and the beans are on top.

10. Serve the frijoles volteados hot as a main dish.

ATOL DE ELOTE

Ingredients:

- Corn - 4 ears
- Water - 4 cups
- Milk - 2 cups
- Sugar - 1/2 cup
- Cinnamon - 1 tsp
- Vanilla - 1 tsp

Instructions:

1. Remove the kernels from the corn and place them in a blender with 2 cups of water.

2. Blend the corn and water until it forms a smooth puree.

3. In a pot, bring the corn puree, milk, sugar, cinnamon, and vanilla to a boil.

4. Reduce the heat to low and let the atol de elote simmer for about 10-15 minutes, stirring occasionally.

5. Serve the atol de elote hot, garnished with a sprinkle of cinnamon and a drizzle of honey if desired.

HILACHAS

Ingredients:

- Beef - 1 pound
- Tomatoes - 2 chopped
- Onion - 1 chopped
- Garlic - 2 cloves
- Cilantro - 1/2 cup chopped
- Salt - to taste

Instructions:

1. Cut the beef into thin strips and season with salt.

2. In a pan, saute the beef strips until browned on all sides.

3. Add the chopped onion, tomatoes, and garlic to the pan and continue to cook until softened.

4. Stir in the chopped cilantro and continue to cook for another 2-3 minutes.

5. Serve the hilachas hot as a main dish with rice or tortillas.

GALLO EN CHICHA

Ingredients:

- Corn - 4 ears
- Water - 4 cups
- Pineapple - 1 peeled and chopped
- Cinnamon - 1 tsp
- Cloves - 5
- Sugar - 1/2 cup

Instructions:

1. Remove the kernels from the corn and place them in a blender with 2 cups of water.

2. Blend the corn and water until it forms a smooth puree.

3. In a pot, bring the corn puree, pineapple, cinnamon, cloves, and sugar to a boil.

4. Reduce the heat to low and let the gallo en chicha simmer for about 20-25 minutes, stirring occasionally.

5. Serve the gallo en chicha hot as a sweet and spicy beverage.

ARROZ CON LECHE

Ingredients:

- Rice - 2 cups
- Water - 4 cups
- Milk - 4 cups
- Sugar - 1/2 cup
- Cinnamon - 1 tsp
- Vanilla - 1 tsp
- Raisins - 1/2 cup

Instructions:

1. Rinse the rice and place it in a pot with 4 cups of water.

2. Add the cinnamon and vanilla to the pot and bring it to a boil.

3. Reduce the heat to low and let the rice simmer for about 20 minutes or until fully cooked and all the liquid has been absorbed.

4. In a separate pot, bring the milk and sugar to a boil.

5. Stir in the cooked rice and raisins, then reduce the heat to low and let the mixture simmer for about 10 minutes.

6. Serve the arroz con leche hot as a sweet and comforting dessert.

TAMALITOS DE CAMBRAY

Ingredients:

- Corn Masa - 2 cups
- Water - 1 cup
- Lard - 1/2 cup
- Baking Powder - 1 tsp
- Salt - to taste
- Cambray - 1 cup chopped
- Tomatoes - 2 chopped
- Onion - 1 chopped
- Garlic - 2 cloves
- Cilantro - 1/2 cup chopped

Instructions:

1. In a large bowl, mix together the corn masa, water, lard, baking powder, and salt until well combined.

2. In a separate pan, saute the chopped cambray, tomatoes, onion, and garlic until softened.

3. Stir in the chopped cilantro and let the mixture cool to

room temperature.

4. Spoon a portion of the masa mixture into each of 12 small corn husks, then add a spoonful of the cambray mixture to the center of each.

5. Fold the husks up and around the filling, securing with kitchen twine if necessary.

6. Place the tamalitos de cambray in a large pot with a steaming basket or insert, then add enough water to the pot to come just below the basket.

7. Cover the pot and bring the water to a boil, then reduce the heat to low and let the tamalitos steam for about 30 minutes or until fully cooked and the masa is tender.

8. Serve the tamalitos de cambray hot as a main dish or as a side to a hearty stew or soup.

ATOL DE ARROZ

Ingredients:

- Rice - 2 cups
- Water - 4 cups
- Milk - 4 cups
- Cinnamon - 1 tsp
- Vanilla - 1 tsp
- Sugar - 1/2 cup
- Raisins - 1/2 cup

Instructions:

1. Rinse the rice and place it in a pot with 4 cups of water.

2. Add the cinnamon and vanilla to the pot and bring it to a boil.

3. Reduce the heat to low and let the rice simmer for about 20 minutes or until fully cooked and all the liquid has been absorbed.

4. In a separate pot, bring the milk, sugar, and raisins to a boil.

5. Stir in the cooked rice, then reduce the heat to low and let the mixture simmer for about 10 minutes.

6. Serve the atol de arroz hot as a sweet and comforting dessert.

PORK

CHICHARRONES

Ingredients:

- Pork skin - 1 pound
- Salt - 1 tablespoon
- Garlic powder - 1 teaspoon
- Onion powder - 1 teaspoon
- Ground cumin - 1 teaspoon
- Dried oregano - 1 teaspoon
- Paprika - 1 teaspoon
- Cayenne pepper - 1/2 teaspoon

Instructions:

1. Preheat the oven to 400°F. Line a baking sheet with parchment paper or aluminum foil.

2. Cut the pork skin into small squares and place them in a large bowl.

3. In a small bowl, mix together the salt, garlic powder, onion powder, cumin, oregano, paprika, and cayenne pepper.

4. Sprinkle the spice mixture over the pork skin and toss to evenly coat.

5. Place the seasoned pork skin on the prepared baking sheet and bake for 20-25 minutes, or until crispy and golden brown. Remove from the oven and let cool for a few minutes before serving.

CARNE ADOBADA

Ingredients:

- Pork shoulder - 2 pounds
- Garlic - 6 cloves, minced
- Apple cider vinegar - 1/2 cup
- Orange juice - 1/2 cup
- Chipotle peppers in adobo sauce - 2 tablespoons, chopped
- Ground cumin - 1 teaspoon
- Ground coriander - 1 teaspoon
- Dried oregano - 1 teaspoon
- Paprika - 1 teaspoon
- Salt - 1 teaspoon
- Black pepper - 1/2 teaspoon

Instructions:

1. In a blender or food processor, combine the garlic, vinegar, orange juice, chipotle peppers, cumin, coriander, oregano, paprika, salt, and pepper. Blend until smooth.

2. Cut the pork shoulder into 1-inch thick slices and place them in a large bowl.

3. Pour the marinade over the pork and toss to evenly coat. Cover and refrigerate for at least 2 hours, or overnight.

4. Preheat a grill or grill pan over medium-high heat.

5. Remove the pork from the marinade and discard any excess marinade.

6. Grill the pork for 5-7 minutes on each side, or until cooked through and slightly charred.

7. Serve the Carne Adobada hot with your favorite sides or in tacos or burritos.

ESTOFADO

Ingredients:

- Pork shoulder - 2 pounds, cut into 1-inch cubes
- Olive oil - 2 tablespoons
- Onion - 1 large, chopped
- Garlic - 4 cloves, minced
- Tomatoes - 2 large, chopped
- Potatoes - 2 medium, peeled and diced
- Carrots - 2 medium, diced
- Chicken broth - 2 cups
- Cilantro - 1/4 cup, chopped
- Salt - 1 teaspoon
- Black pepper - 1/2 teaspoon

Instructions:

1. In a large saucepan or Dutch oven, heat the olive oil over medium heat.

2. Add the onion and cook until softened, about 5 minutes.

3. Add the garlic and cook for another minute, or until fragrant.

4. Add the pork and cook until browned on all sides, about 5-7 minutes.

5. Add the tomatoes, potatoes, carrots, broth, cilantro, salt, and pepper to the pan.

6. Stir to combine and bring to a boil.

7. Reduce the heat to low, cover, and simmer for 45 minutes, or until the pork is tender and the vegetables are cooked through.

8. Serve the Estofado hot with crusty bread or over rice.

REVOLCADO

Ingredients:

- Pork shoulder - 2 pounds, cut into 1-inch cubes
- Tomatoes - 4 large, chopped
- Onion - 1 large, chopped
- Garlic - 4 cloves, minced
- Bell peppers - 2 medium, chopped
- Jalapeño peppers - 2, seeded and chopped
- Cumin - 1 teaspoon
- Oregano - 1 teaspoon
- Paprika - 1 teaspoon
- Salt - 1 teaspoon
- Black pepper - 1/2 teaspoon

Instructions:

1. In a large skillet, heat some oil over medium heat.

2. Add the pork and cook until browned on all sides, about 5-7 minutes.

3. Remove the pork from the skillet and set aside.

4. In the same skillet, add the tomatoes, onion, garlic, bell peppers, jalapeño peppers, cumin, oregano, paprika, salt, and pepper.

5. Cook until the vegetables are softened, about 5-7 minutes.

6. Return the pork to the skillet and stir to combine with the vegetables.

7. Cover the skillet and simmer for 20-25 minutes, or until the pork is tender and the sauce has thickened.

8. Serve the Revolcado hot with rice or tortillas.

LOMITOS DE CERDO

Ingredients:

- Pork tenderloin - 2 pounds, sliced into 1/2-inch thick medallions
- Flour - 1 cup
- Salt - 1 teaspoon
- Black pepper - 1/2 teaspoon
- Eggs - 2, beaten
- Breadcrumbs - 1 cup
- Olive oil - 1/4 cup

Instructions:

1. In a shallow dish, mix together the flour, salt, and pepper.

2. In another shallow dish, beat the eggs.

3. In a third shallow dish, place the breadcrumbs.

4. Dip each pork medallion in the flour mixture, then in the beaten eggs, and finally in the breadcrumbs, making sure to coat well.

5. In a large skillet, heat the olive oil over medium heat.

6. Add the pork medallions to the skillet and cook for 3-4

minutes on each side, or until golden brown and cooked through.

7. Serve the Lomitos de Cerdo hot with your favorite sides or sauces.

LONGANIZA

Ingredients:

- Ground pork - 2 pounds
- Garlic - 4 cloves, minced
- White vinegar - 2 tablespoons
- Sugar - 1 tablespoon
- Ancho chili powder - 1 tablespoon
- Ground cumin - 1 teaspoon
- Ground coriander - 1 teaspoon
- Dried oregano - 1 teaspoon
- Paprika - 1 teaspoon
- Salt - 1 teaspoon
- Black pepper - 1/2 teaspoon

Instructions:

1. In a large bowl, mix together the ground pork, garlic, vinegar, sugar, chili powder, cumin, coriander, oregano, paprika, salt, and pepper.

2. Cover the bowl and refrigerate for at least 2 hours, or overnight.

3. Preheat a grill or grill pan over medium-high heat.

4. Divide the pork mixture into 8 portions and shape each portion into a sausage shape.

5. Place the sausages on the grill or grill pan and cook for

8-10 minutes, or until browned on all sides and cooked through.

6. Serve the Longaniza hot with corn tortillas, salsa, and avocado or in tacos or burritos.

TAMALES COLORADOS

Ingredients:

- Pork shoulder - 2 pounds, cooked and shredded
- Tomatoes - 4 large, chopped
- Onion - 1 large, chopped
- Garlic - 4 cloves, minced
- Ancho chili powder - 2 tablespoons
- Ground cumin - 1 teaspoon
- Dried oregano - 1 teaspoon
- Salt - 1 teaspoon
- Black pepper - 1/2 teaspoon
- Corn husks - 24, soaked in warm water for 30 minutes
- Masa harina - 2 cups
- Lard or vegetable shortening - 1 cup, melted
- Chicken broth - 1 cup

Instructions:

1. In a large saucepan, heat some oil over medium heat.

2. Add the onion and cook until softened, about 5 minutes.

3. Add the garlic and cook for another minute, or until fragrant.

4. Add the tomatoes, chili powder, cumin, oregano, salt, and pepper to the pan. Cook until the sauce has

thickened, about 10 minutes.

5. Add the shredded pork to the sauce and stir to combine.

6. In a large bowl, mix together the masa harina, lard or shortening, and chicken broth until a smooth dough forms.

7. To assemble the tamales, spread a spoonful of the dough onto a soaked corn husk, leaving about 2 inches at the bottom and 1 inch at the top uncovered. Spoon some of the pork mixture onto the center of the dough.

8. Roll up the corn husk tightly around the filling, tucking in the sides as you go.

9. Repeat with the remaining dough and filling.

10. Place the tamales in a steamer basket and steam for 45-50 minutes, or until the dough is cooked through and the tamales are firm to the touch.

11. Serve the Tamales Colorados hot with extra sauce on the side.

CERDO EN ACHIOTE

Ingredients:

- Pork shoulder - 2 pounds, cut into 1-inch cubes
- Achiote paste - 1/4 cup
- Orange juice - 1/2 cup
- Lime juice - 1/2 cup
- Garlic - 4 cloves, minced
- Cumin - 1 teaspoon
- Oregano - 1 teaspoon

- Salt - 1 teaspoon
- Black pepper - 1/2 teaspoon

Instructions:

1. In a large bowl, mix together the achiote paste, orange juice, lime juice, garlic, cumin, oregano, salt, and pepper.

2. Add the pork to the bowl and stir to coat with the marinade.

3. Cover the bowl and refrigerate for at least 2 hours, or overnight.

4. Preheat a grill or grill pan over medium-high heat.

5. Place the pork on the grill or grill pan and cook for 8-10 minutes, or until browned on all sides and cooked through.

6. Serve the Cerdo en Achiote hot with rice, beans, and tortillas.

MORONGA

Ingredients:

- Pork blood - 1 cup
- Pork liver - 1/2 pound, chopped
- Onion - 1 large, chopped
- Garlic - 4 cloves, minced
- Tomatoes - 2 large, chopped
- Cilantro - 1/4 cup, chopped
- Ancho chili powder - 1 tablespoon
- Ground cumin - 1 teaspoon
- Salt - 1 teaspoon
- Black pepper - 1/2 teaspoon

Instructions:

1. In a large saucepan, heat some oil over medium heat.

2. Add the onion and cook until softened, about 5 minutes.

3. Add the garlic and cook for another minute, or until fragrant.

4. Add the pork liver and cook until browned, about 5-7 minutes.

5. Add the tomatoes, cilantro, chili powder, cumin, salt, and pepper to the pan.

6. Stir to combine and cook until the sauce has thickened, about 10 minutes.

7. Stir in the pork blood and cook until heated through, about 2-3 minutes.

8. Serve the Moronga hot with rice, beans, and tortillas.

CERDO CON VERDURAS

Ingredients:

- Pork shoulder - 2 pounds, cut into 1-inch cubes
- Potatoes - 2 large, diced
- Carrots - 2 large, diced
- Onion - 1 large, chopped
- Garlic - 4 cloves, minced
- Tomatoes - 2 large, chopped
- Bell peppers - 2, diced
- Cumin - 1 teaspoon
- Oregano - 1 teaspoon

- Salt - 1 teaspoon
- Black pepper - 1/2 teaspoon

Instructions:

1. In a large skillet, heat some oil over medium heat.

2. Add the onion and cook until softened, about 5 minutes.

3. Add the garlic and cook for another minute, or until fragrant.

4. Add the pork to the skillet and cook until browned on all sides, about 8-10 minutes.

5. Add the potatoes, carrots, tomatoes, bell peppers, cumin, oregano, salt, and pepper to the skillet.

6. Stir to combine and cover the skillet.

7. Simmer for 20-25 minutes, or until the pork is tender and the vegetables are cooked through.

8. Serve the Cerdo con Verduras hot with rice or tortillas.

CERDO EN PIPIAN

Ingredients:

- Pork shoulder - 2 pounds, cut into 1-inch cubes
- Tomatoes - 4 large, chopped
- Sesame seeds - 1/4 cup
- Pumpkin seeds - 1/4 cup
- Peanuts - 1/4 cup
- Garlic - 4 cloves
- Ancho chili powder - 2 tablespoons

- Cumin - 1 teaspoon
- Oregano - 1 teaspoon
- Salt - 1 teaspoon
- Black pepper - 1/2 teaspoon

Instructions:

1. In a large saucepan, heat some oil over medium heat.

2. Add the tomatoes and cook until softened, about 5 minutes.

3. Add the sesame seeds, pumpkin seeds, peanuts, garlic, chili powder, cumin, oregano, salt, and pepper to the pan.

4. Cook for another 2-3 minutes, or until fragrant and the seeds are toasted.

5. Transfer the mixture to a blender and blend until smooth.

6. Return the sauce to the saucepan and bring to a simmer.

7. Add the pork to the sauce and stir to coat with the sauce.

8. Cover the saucepan and simmer for 20-25 minutes, or until the pork is tender and cooked through.

9. Serve the Cerdo en Pipian hot with rice or tortillas.

CERDO EN JOCON

Ingredients:

- Pork shoulder - 2 pounds, cut into 1-inch cubes

- Tomatoes - 4 large, chopped
- Tomatillos - 4, chopped
- Jalapeno peppers - 2, seeded and chopped
- Garlic - 4 cloves, minced
- Cilantro - 1/4 cup, chopped
- Ancho chili powder - 2 tablespoons
- Ground cumin - 1 teaspoon
- Oregano - 1 teaspoon
- Salt - 1 teaspoon
- Black pepper - 1/2 teaspoon

Instructions:

1. In a large saucepan, heat some oil over medium heat.

2. Add the onions and cook until softened, about 5 minutes.

3. Add the garlic and cook for another minute, or until fragrant.

4. Add the tomatoes, tomatillos, jalapeno peppers, cilantro, chili powder, cumin, oregano, salt, and pepper to the pan.

5. Cook until the sauce has thickened, about 10 minutes.

6. Add the pork to the sauce and stir to coat with the sauce.

7. Cover the saucepan and simmer for 20-25 minutes, or until the pork is tender and cooked through.

8. Serve the Cerdo en Jocon hot with rice or tortillas.

CERDO EN KAK'IK

Ingredients:

- Pork shoulder - 2 pounds, cut into 1-inch cubes
- Tomatoes - 4 large, chopped
- Guajillo chili peppers - 4, seeded and chopped
- Garlic - 4 cloves, minced
- Coriander - 1/4 cup, chopped
- Cumin - 1 teaspoon
- Oregano - 1 teaspoon
- Salt - 1 teaspoon
- Black pepper - 1/2 teaspoon

Instructions:

1. In a large saucepan, heat some oil over medium heat.

2. Add the tomatoes and cook until softened, about 5 minutes.

3. Add the guajillo chili peppers, garlic, coriander, cumin, oregano, salt, and pepper to the pan.

4. Cook for another 2-3 minutes, or until fragrant.

5. Transfer the mixture to a blender and blend until smooth.

6. Return the sauce to the saucepan and bring to a simmer.

7. Add the pork to the sauce and stir to coat with the sauce.

8. Cover the saucepan and simmer for 20-25 minutes, or until the pork is tender and cooked through.

9. Serve the Cerdo en Kak'ik hot with rice or tortillas.

CHORIZO

Ingredients:

- Pork shoulder - 2 pounds, ground
- Paprika - 2 tablespoons
- Garlic - 4 cloves, minced
- Cumin - 1 teaspoon
- Oregano - 1 teaspoon
- Salt - 1 teaspoon
- Black pepper - 1/2 teaspoon

Instructions:

1. In a large bowl, mix together the ground pork, paprika, garlic, cumin, oregano, salt, and pepper.

2. Cover the bowl and refrigerate for at least 2 hours, or overnight.

3. In a large skillet, heat some oil over medium heat.

4. Add the pork mixture to the skillet and cook, breaking it up into small pieces with a wooden spoon, until browned and cooked through, about 10-15 minutes.

5. Serve the Chorizo hot with eggs, potatoes, or in tacos or burritos.

CERDO EN SALSA DE TOMATE

Ingredients:

- Pork shoulder - 2 pounds, cut into 1-inch cubes
- Tomatoes - 4 large, chopped

- Onion - 1 large, chopped
- Garlic - 4 cloves, minced
- Cilantro - 1/4 cup, chopped
- Cumin - 1 teaspoon
- Oregano - 1 teaspoon
- Salt - 1 teaspoon
- Black pepper - 1/2 teaspoon

Instructions:

1. In a large saucepan, heat some oil over medium heat.

2. Add the onion and cook until softened, about 5 minutes.

3. Add the garlic and cook for another minute, or until fragrant.

4. Add the tomatoes, cilantro, cumin, oregano, salt, and pepper to the pan. Cook until the sauce has thickened, about 10 minutes.

5. Add the pork to the sauce and stir to coat with the sauce.

6. Cover the saucepan and simmer for 20-25 minutes, or until the pork is tender and cooked through.

7. Serve the Cerdo en Salsa de Tomate hot with rice or tortillas.

BEEF

BISTEC ENCEBOLLADO

Ingredients:

- Beef Steak - 1 lb
- Onions - 2, sliced
- Garlic - 4 cloves, minced
- Tomato Sauce - 1 cup
- Oregano - 1 tsp
- Salt - to taste
- Pepper - to taste
- Olive Oil - 1/4 cup

Instructions:

1. In a large skillet, heat olive oil over medium heat. Add sliced onions and cook until soft and translucent, about 5 minutes.

2. Add minced garlic and cook for an additional minute.

3. Add the beef steaks to the skillet and cook until browned on both sides, about 4 minutes per side.

4. Stir in the tomato sauce, oregano, salt, and pepper. Bring to a simmer and let cook for an additional 10 minutes or until the sauce has thickened slightly.

5. Serve the steaks topped with the onion and tomato sauce.

HILACHAS

Ingredients:

- Shredded Beef - 1 lb
- Tomatoes - 2, diced
- Onions - 1, diced
- Garlic - 3 cloves, minced
- Cumin - 1 tsp
- Oregano - 1 tsp
- Salt - to taste
- Pepper - to taste
- Tortillas - 8

Instructions:

1. In a large skillet, heat a little bit of oil over medium heat. Add diced onions and cook until soft and translucent, about 5 minutes.

2. Add minced garlic and cook for an additional minute.

3. Add the shredded beef to the skillet and cook until heated through, about 4 minutes.

4. Stir in the diced tomatoes, cumin, oregano, salt, and pepper. Let cook for an additional 5 minutes or until the sauce has thickened slightly.

5. Serve the hilachas with warm tortillas.

CARNE GUISADA

Ingredients:

- Beef Stew Meat - 1 lb
- Potatoes - 2, diced

- Carrots - 2, diced
- Tomatoes - 2, diced
- Onions - 1, diced
- Garlic - 3 cloves, minced
- Cumin - 1 tsp
- Oregano - 1 tsp
- Salt - to taste
- Pepper - to taste
- Water - 2 cups

Instructions:

1. In a large pot, heat a little bit of oil over medium heat. Add diced onions and cook until soft and translucent, about 5 minutes.

2. Add minced garlic and cook for an additional minute.

3. Add the beef stew meat to the pot and cook until browned on all sides, about 4 minutes per side.

4. Stir in the diced potatoes, carrots, tomatoes, cumin, oregano, salt, and pepper. Add water and bring to a boil.

5. Reduce heat to low, cover the pot, and let simmer for 1 hour or until the meat is tender and the sauce has thickened.

6. Serve the carne guisada hot with rice or tortillas.

LENGUA EN SALSA

Ingredients:

- Beef Tongue - 1 lb
- Tomatoes - 2, diced
- Onions - 1, diced

- Garlic - 3 cloves, minced
- Cumin - 1 tsp
- Oregano - 1 tsp
- Salt - to taste
- Pepper - to taste
- Water - 2 cups

Instructions:

1. In a large pot, add the beef tongue and enough water to cover. Bring to a boil and let cook for 1 hour or until the tongue is tender.

2. Remove the tongue from the pot and let cool. Once cooled, peel the skin and dice the tongue into small pieces.

3. In a large skillet, heat a little bit of oil over medium heat. Add diced onions and cook until soft and translucent, about 5 minutes.

4. Add minced garlic and cook for an additional minute.

5. Add the diced tongue to the skillet and cook until heated through, about 4 minutes.

6. Stir in the diced tomatoes, cumin, oregano, salt, and pepper. Let cook for an additional 5 minutes or until the sauce has thickened slightly.

7. Serve the lengua en salsa hot with rice or tortillas.

BISTEC CHAPIN

Ingredients:

- Beef Steak - 1 lb

- Tomatoes - 2, diced
- Onions - 1, diced
- Green Bell Pepper - 1, diced
- Garlic - 3 cloves, minced
- Cumin - 1 tsp
- Oregano - 1 tsp
- Salt - to taste
- Pepper - to taste
- Lemon Juice - 2 tbsp
- Olive Oil - 1/4 cup

Instructions:

1. In a large skillet, heat olive oil over medium heat. Add diced onions and cook until soft and translucent, about 5 minutes.

2. Add minced garlic and cook for an additional minute.

3. Add the beef steaks to the skillet and cook until browned on both sides, about 4 minutes per side.

4. Stir in the diced tomatoes, green bell pepper, cumin, oregano, salt, and pepper. Let cook for an additional 5 minutes.

5. Remove the steaks from the skillet and set aside. Add lemon juice to the skillet and let cook for another minute.

6. Serve the bistec chapin topped with the tomato and green pepper sauce.

TAMALES NEGROS

Ingredients:

- Corn Masa - 2 lbs

- Black Beans - 1 cup, mashed
- Dried Ancho Chiles - 4, rehydrated and blended
- Garlic - 4 cloves, minced
- Cumin - 1 tsp
- Oregano - 1 tsp
- Salt - to taste
- Pepper - to taste
- Corn Husks - 20

Instructions:

1. In a large bowl, mix together the corn masa, mashed black beans, blended ancho chiles, minced garlic, cumin, oregano, salt, and pepper.

2. Soak the corn husks in warm water for 30 minutes to soften.

3. Spoon a large spoonful of the masa mixture onto the center of each corn husk and spread evenly to cover about 2/3 of the husk.

4. Roll up the husk, tucking in the sides as you go, to form a tight cylinder. Repeat with the remaining masa and husks.

5. Place the tamales in a large pot with a steamer basket. Add enough water to the pot to reach the bottom of the steamer basket. Cover and steam the tamales for 1 hour or until the masa is fully cooked and the tamales are heated through.

6. Serve the tamales negros hot with salsa or a side of rice.

SALPICON DE RES

Ingredients:

- Shredded Beef - 1 lb
- Tomatoes - 2, diced
- Onions - 1, diced
- Green Bell Pepper - 1, diced
- Jalapeno Pepper - 1, diced
- Cilantro - 1/4 cup, chopped
- Lemon Juice - 2 tbsp
- Salt - to taste
- Pepper - to taste

Instructions:

1. In a large bowl, mix together the shredded beef, diced tomatoes, onions, green bell pepper, jalapeno pepper, cilantro, lemon juice, salt, and pepper.

2. Cover the bowl and refrigerate for at least 30 minutes to allow the flavors to meld together.

3. Serve the salpicon de res cold as a salad or as a filling for tacos or burritos.

PICADILLO

Ingredients:

- Ground Beef - 1 lb
- Tomatoes - 2, diced
- Onions - 1, diced
- Garlic - 3 cloves, minced
- Green Olives - 1/2 cup, chopped
- Raisins - 1/2 cup
- Cumin - 1 tsp

- Oregano - 1 tsp
- Salt - to taste
- Pepper - to taste

Instructions:

1. In a large skillet, heat a little bit of oil over medium heat. Add diced onions and cook until soft and translucent, about 5 minutes.

2. Add minced garlic and cook for an additional minute.

3. Add the ground beef to the skillet and cook until browned, about 4 minutes.

4. Stir in the diced tomatoes, green olives, raisins, cumin, oregano, salt, and pepper. Let cook for an additional 5 minutes or until the sauce has thickened slightly.

5. Serve the picadillo hot with rice or as a filling for tacos or burritos.

ROPA VIEJA

Ingredients:

- Shredded Beef - 1 lb
- Tomatoes - 2, diced
- Onions - 1, diced
- Green Bell Pepper - 1, diced
- Garlic - 3 cloves, minced
- Cumin - 1 tsp
- Oregano - 1 tsp
- Salt - to taste
- Pepper - to taste
- Water - 2 cups

Instructions:

1. In a large pot, heat a little bit of oil over medium heat. Add diced onions and cook until soft and translucent, about 5 minutes.

2. Add minced garlic and cook for an additional minute.

3. Add the shredded beef to the pot and cook until heated through, about 4 minutes.

4. Stir in the diced tomatoes, green bell pepper, cumin, oregano, salt, and pepper. Add water and bring to a boil.

5. Reduce heat to low, cover the pot, and let simmer for 30 minutes or until the sauce has thickened.

6. Serve the ropa vieja hot with rice or tortillas.

CALDO DE COSTILLA

Ingredients:

- Beef Ribs - 1 lb
- Potatoes - 2, diced
- Carrots - 2, diced
- Onions - 1, diced
- Garlic - 3 cloves, minced
- Cumin - 1 tsp
- Oregano - 1 tsp
- Salt - to taste
- Pepper - to taste
- Water - 4 cups

Instructions:

1. In a large pot, add the beef ribs and enough water to

cover. Bring to a boil and let cook for 1 hour or until the ribs are tender.

2. Remove the ribs from the pot and let cool. Once cooled, cut the ribs into individual pieces.

3. In the same pot, add the diced potatoes, carrots, and onions. Bring to a boil and let cook for 15 minutes or until the vegetables are tender.

4. Stir in the minced garlic, cumin, oregano, salt, and pepper. Let cook for an additional minute.

5. Return the rib pieces to the pot and add additional water if needed to cover the ingredients. Bring to a boil and let cook for 10 minutes or until heated through.

6. Serve the caldo de costilla hot as a soup or over rice.

ALBONDIGAS GUATEMALTECAS

Ingredients:

- Ground Beef - 1 lb
- Breadcrumbs - 1/2 cup
- Onions - 1/2, diced
- Garlic - 3 cloves, minced
- Eggs - 1
- Cilantro - 1/4 cup, chopped
- Cumin - 1 tsp
- Oregano - 1 tsp
- Salt - to taste
- Pepper - to taste
- Water - 4 cups

Instructions:

1. In a large bowl, mix together the ground beef, breadcrumbs, diced onions, minced garlic, eggs, cilantro, cumin, oregano, salt, and pepper.

2. Using your hands, form the mixture into small meatballs, about 1.5 inches in diameter.

3. In a large pot, bring the water to a boil. Add the meatballs to the pot and let cook for 10-12 minutes or until fully cooked and heated through.

4. Serve the albondigas guatemaltecas hot with rice or in a broth as a soup.

CARNE ASADA

Ingredients:

- Beef Steaks - 4
- Lime Juice - 1/2 cup
- Garlic - 4 cloves, minced
- Cumin - 1 tsp
- Oregano - 1 tsp
- Salt - to taste
- Pepper - to taste
- Olive Oil - 1/4 cup

Instructions:

1. In a large bowl, mix together the lime juice, minced garlic, cumin, oregano, salt, and pepper. Add the beef steaks to the bowl and let marinate for at least 30 minutes in the refrigerator.

2. In a large skillet, heat the olive oil over medium heat. Add the marinated steaks and cook until browned on both sides, about 4 minutes per side.

3. Serve the carne asada hot with your favorite sides or as a filling for tacos or burritos.

ESTOFADO DE RES

Ingredients:

- Beef Stew Meat - 1 lb
- Tomatoes - 2, diced
- Onions - 1, diced
- Garlic - 3 cloves, minced
- Carrots - 2, diced
- Potatoes - 2, diced
- Cumin - 1 tsp
- Oregano - 1 tsp
- Salt - to taste
- Pepper - to taste
- Water - 2 cups

Instructions:

1. In a large pot, heat a little bit of oil over medium heat. Add diced onions and cook until soft and translucent, about 5 minutes.

2. Add minced garlic and cook for an additional minute.

3. Add the beef stew meat to the pot and cook until browned, about 4 minutes.

4. Stir in the diced tomatoes, carrots, potatoes, cumin, oregano, salt, and pepper. Add water and bring to a boil.

5. Reduce heat to low, cover the pot, and let simmer for 1 hour or until the beef is tender and the sauce has thickened.

6. Serve the estofado de res hot with rice or over crusty bread.

CARNE EN JOCON

Ingredients:

- Beef Stew Meat - 1 lb
- Tomatoes - 2, diced
- Onions - 1, diced
- Garlic - 3 cloves, minced
- Jalapeno Pepper - 1, diced
- Tomatillo - 1, diced
- Cilantro - 1/4 cup, chopped
- Cumin - 1 tsp
- Oregano - 1 tsp
- Salt - to taste
- Pepper - to taste
- Water - 2 cups

Instructions:

1. In a large pot, heat a little bit of oil over medium heat. Add diced onions and cook until soft and translucent, about 5 minutes.

2. Add minced garlic and cook for an additional minute.

3. Add the beef stew meat to the pot and cook until browned, about 4 minutes.

4. Stir in the diced tomatoes, jalapeno pepper, tomatillo, cilantro, cumin, oregano, salt, and pepper. Add water and bring to a boil.

5. Reduce heat to low, cover the pot, and let simmer for 1 hour or until the beef is tender and the sauce has

thickened.

6. Serve the carne en jocon hot with rice or over crusty bread.

MILANESA DE RES

Ingredients:

- Beef Cutlets - 4
- Eggs - 2
- Breadcrumbs - 1 cup
- Salt - to taste
- Pepper - to taste
- Olive Oil - 1/4 cup

Instructions:

1. In a shallow dish, beat the eggs with a little bit of salt and pepper.

2. In another shallow dish, spread the breadcrumbs evenly.

3. Dip each beef cutlet into the beaten eggs and then into the breadcrumbs, pressing the breadcrumbs onto the cutlets to make sure they adhere well.

4. In a large skillet, heat the olive oil over medium heat. Add the breaded beef cutlets to the skillet and cook until browned on both sides, about 4 minutes per side.

5. Serve the milanesa de res hot with your favorite sides or as a filling for sandwiches or tacos.

CHICKEN

POLLO EN PEPIAN

Ingredients:

- Chicken - 1 whole
- Tomatoes - 4
- Onions - 2
- Garlic - 3 cloves
- Tomatillos - 6
- Coriander - 1/4 cup
- Sesame seeds - 1/4 cup
- Cumin - 1 tsp
- Pepper - 1 tsp
- Salt - 1 tsp

Instructions:

1. In a saucepan, cook the chicken until fully cooked. Remove from heat and let cool.

2. In a blender, puree the tomatoes, onions, garlic, tomatillos, coriander, sesame seeds, cumin, pepper, and salt.

3. In a large skillet, heat a few tablespoons of oil over medium heat. Add the pureed mixture and cook for 10 minutes.

4. Add the cooked chicken to the skillet and cover with the sauce. Cook for an additional 10 minutes.

5. Serve hot with rice or tortillas.

POLLO EN JOCON

Ingredients:

- Chicken - 1 whole
- Tomatoes - 4
- Onions - 2
- Garlic - 3 cloves
- Green bell peppers - 2
- Tomatillos - 6
- Coriander - 1/4 cup
- Chicken broth - 2 cups
- Jalapeno peppers - 2
- Cumin - 1 tsp
- Pepper - 1 tsp
- Salt - 1 tsp

Instructions:

1. In a saucepan, cook the chicken until fully cooked. Remove from heat and let cool.

2. In a blender, puree the tomatoes, onions, garlic, green bell peppers, tomatillos, coriander, chicken broth, jalapeno peppers, cumin, pepper, and salt.

3. In a large skillet, heat a few tablespoons of oil over medium heat. Add the pureed mixture and cook for 10 minutes.

4. Add the cooked chicken to the skillet and cover with the sauce. Cook for an additional 10 minutes.

5. Serve hot with rice or tortillas.

POLLO EN SALSA

Ingredients:

- Chicken - 1 whole
- Tomatoes - 4
- Onions - 2
- Garlic - 3 cloves
- Green bell peppers - 2
- Coriander - 1/4 cup
- Chicken broth - 2 cups
- Jalapeno peppers - 2
- Cumin - 1 tsp
- Pepper - 1 tsp
- Salt - 1 tsp

Instructions:

1. In a saucepan, cook the chicken until fully cooked. Remove from heat and let cool.

2. In a blender, puree the tomatoes, onions, garlic, green bell peppers, coriander, chicken broth, jalapeno peppers, cumin, pepper, and salt.

3. In a large skillet, heat a few tablespoons of oil over medium heat. Add the pureed mixture and cook for 10 minutes.

4. Add the cooked chicken to the skillet and cover with the sauce. Cook for an additional 10 minutes.

5. Serve hot with rice or tortillas.

POLLO EN ESCABECHE

Ingredients:

- Chicken - 1 whole
- Onions - 2
- Garlic - 3 cloves
- Carrots - 2
- Vinegar - 1 cup
- Coriander - 1/4 cup
- Pepper - 1 tsp
- Salt - 1 tsp

Instructions:

1. In a saucepan, cook the chicken until fully cooked. Remove from heat and let cool.

2. In a large skillet, heat a few tablespoons of oil over medium heat. Add the onions, garlic, and carrots and cook until softened.

3. Add the vinegar, coriander, pepper, and salt to the skillet and stir to combine.

4. Add the cooked chicken to the skillet and cover with the escabeche mixture. Cook for an additional 10 minutes.

5. Serve hot with rice or tortillas.

POLLO GUISADO

Ingredients:

- Chicken - 1 whole
- Tomatoes - 4

- Onions - 2
- Garlic - 3 cloves
- Potatoes - 2
- Carrots - 2
- Coriander
- Chicken broth - 2 cups
- Cumin - 1 tsp
- Pepper - 1 tsp
- Salt - 1 tsp

Instructions:

1. In a saucepan, cook the chicken until fully cooked. Remove from heat and let cool.

2. In a large skillet, heat a few tablespoons of oil over medium heat. Add the onions, garlic, potatoes, and carrots and cook until softened.

3. Add the tomatoes, chicken broth, cumin, pepper, and salt to the skillet and stir to combine.

4. Add the cooked chicken to the skillet and cover with the guisado mixture. Cook for an additional 10 minutes.

5. Serve hot with rice or tortillas.

POLLO FRITO

Ingredients:

- Chicken - 1 whole
- Flour - 1 cup
- Eggs - 2
- Breadcrumbs - 1 cup
- Pepper - 1 tsp
- Salt - 1 tsp

- Oil for frying

Instructions:

1. Cut the chicken into small pieces.

2. In a shallow dish, mix the flour, pepper, and salt.

3. In another shallow dish, beat the eggs.

4. In a third shallow dish, place the breadcrumbs.

5. Dip each chicken piece into the flour mixture, then into the eggs, and finally into the breadcrumbs, making sure each piece is fully coated.

6. In a large skillet, heat a few inches of oil over medium heat. Fry the chicken pieces until golden brown on both sides, about 5 minutes per side.

7. Serve hot with your favorite dipping sauce.

POLLO ASADO

Ingredients:

- Chicken - 1 whole
- Lemon - 1
- Garlic - 3 cloves
- Oregano - 1 tsp
- Pepper - 1 tsp
- Salt - 1 tsp

Instructions:

1. Preheat your oven to 400°F.

2. In a small bowl, mix the lemon juice, minced garlic, oregano, pepper, and salt to make a marinade.

3. Place the chicken in a large baking dish and pour the marinade over the chicken, making sure to fully coat the chicken.

4. Bake the chicken in the oven for 35-40 minutes, or until the internal temperature reaches 165°F.

5. Remove from oven and let cool for a few minutes before serving.

POLLO A LA CERVEZA

Ingredients:

- Chicken - 1 whole
- Beer - 1 bottle
- Lemon - 1
- Garlic - 3 cloves
- Oregano - 1 tsp
- Pepper - 1 tsp
- Salt - 1 tsp

Instructions:

1. Preheat your oven to 400°F.

2. In a large baking dish, place the chicken and pour the beer over the chicken.

3. Squeeze the lemon over the chicken and place the lemon halves inside the chicken cavity.

4. Add the minced garlic, oregano, pepper, and salt to the baking dish and mix to combine.

5. Bake the chicken in the oven for 35-40 minutes, or until the internal temperature reaches 165°F.

6. Remove from oven and let cool for a few minutes before serving.

POLLO CON LOROCO

Ingredients:

- Chicken - 1 whole
- Loroco - 1 cup
- Onions - 2
- Garlic - 3 cloves
- Tomatoes - 4
- Chicken broth - 2 cups
- Cumin - 1 tsp
- Pepper - 1 tsp
- Salt - 1 tsp

Instructions:

1. In a saucepan, cook the chicken until fully cooked. Remove from heat and let cool.

2. In a large skillet, heat a few tablespoons of oil over medium heat. Add the onions and garlic and cook until softened.

3. Add the loroco, tomatoes, chicken broth, cumin, pepper, and salt to the skillet and stir to combine.

4. Add the cooked chicken to the skillet and cover with the loroco mixture. Cook for an additional 10 minutes.

5. Serve hot with rice or tortillas.

POLLO EN SUBANIK

Ingredients:

- Chicken - 1 whole
- Tomatoes - 4
- Onions - 2
- Garlic - 3 cloves
- Coriander - 1/4 cup
- Chicken broth - 2 cups
- Chile Pasilla - 2
- Cumin - 1 tsp
- Pepper - 1 tsp
- Salt - 1 tsp

Instructions:

1. In a saucepan, cook the chicken until fully cooked. Remove from heat and let cool.

2. In a blender, puree the tomatoes, onions, garlic, coriander, chicken broth, pasilla peppers, cumin, pepper, and salt.

3. In a large skillet, heat a few tablespoons of oil over medium heat. Add the pureed mixture and cook for 10 minutes.

4. Add the cooked chicken to the skillet and cover with the sauce. Cook for an additional 10 minutes.

5. Serve hot with rice or tortillas.

POLLO EN KAK'IK

Ingredients:

- Chicken - 1 whole
- Tomatoes - 4
- Onions - 2
- Garlic - 3 cloves
- Chile Ancho - 2
- Chile Guajillo - 2
- Chicken broth - 2 cups
- Coriander - 1/4 cup
- Cumin - 1 tsp
- Pepper - 1 tsp
- Salt - 1 tsp

Instructions:

1. In a saucepan, cook the chicken until fully cooked. Remove from heat and let cool.

2. In a blender, puree the tomatoes, onions, garlic, ancho peppers, guajillo peppers, chicken broth, coriander, cumin, pepper, and salt.

3. In a large skillet, heat a few tablespoons of oil over medium heat. Add the pureed mixture and cook for 10 minutes.

4. Add the cooked chicken to the skillet and cover with the sauce. Cook for an additional 10 minutes.

5. Serve hot with rice or tortillas.

POLLO EN CHICHA

Ingredients:

- Chicken - 1 whole
- Tomatoes - 4
- Onions - 2
- Garlic - 3 cloves
- Chicha - 1 cup
- Coriander - 1/4 cup
- Cumin - 1 tsp
- Pepper - 1 tsp
- Salt - 1 tsp

Instructions:

1. In a saucepan, cook the chicken until fully cooked. Remove from heat and let cool.

2. In a blender, puree the tomatoes, onions, garlic, coriander, chicha, cumin, pepper, and salt.

3. In a large skillet, heat a few tablespoons of oil over medium heat. Add the pureed mixture and cook for 10 minutes.

4. Add the cooked chicken to the skillet and cover with the sauce. Cook for an additional 10 minutes.

5. Serve hot with rice or tortillas.

POLLO EN ACHIOTE

Ingredients:

- Chicken - 1 whole
- Achiote paste - 1/4 cup

- Lemon - 1
- Garlic - 3 cloves
- Oregano - 1 tsp
- Pepper - 1 tsp
- Salt - 1 tsp

Instructions:

1. Preheat your oven to 400°F.

2. In a small bowl, mix the achiote paste, lemon juice, minced garlic, oregano, pepper, and salt to make a marinade.

3. Place the chicken in a large baking dish and pour the marinade over the chicken, making sure to fully coat the chicken.

4. Bake the chicken in the oven for 35-40 minutes, or until the internal temperature reaches 165°F.

5. Remove from oven and let cool for a few minutes before serving.

POLLO AL HORNO

Ingredients:

- Chicken - 1 whole
- Lemon - 1
- Garlic - 3 cloves
- Oregano - 1 tsp
- Pepper - 1 tsp
- Salt - 1 tsp

Instructions:

1. Preheat your oven to 400°F.

2. In a small bowl, mix the lemon juice, minced garlic, oregano, pepper, and salt to make a marinade.

3. Place the chicken in a large baking dish and pour the marinade over the chicken, making sure to fully coat the chicken.

4. Bake the chicken in the oven for 35-40 minutes, or until the internal temperature reaches 165°F.

5. Remove from oven and let cool for a few minutes before serving.

POLLO ENCEBOLLADO

Ingredients:

- Chicken - 1 whole
- Onions - 2
- Garlic - 3 cloves
- Tomatoes - 4
- Chicken broth - 2 cups
- Oregano - 1 tsp
- Pepper - 1 tsp
- Salt - 1 tsp

Instructions:

1. In a saucepan, cook the chicken until fully cooked. Remove from heat and let cool.

2. In a large skillet, heat a few tablespoons of oil over medium heat. Add the onions and garlic and cook until softened.

3. Add the diced tomatoes, chicken broth, oregano, pepper, and salt to the skillet and stir to combine.

4. Add the cooked chicken to the skillet and cover with the sauce. Cook for an additional 10 minutes.

5. Serve hot with rice or tortillas.

SEAFOOD

CEVICHE CHAPIN

Ingredients:

- Fish - 1 lb
- Lemon Juice - 1 cup
- Red Onion - 1
- Tomatoes - 2
- Cilantro - 1/2 cup
- Jalapeno Pepper - 1
- Salt - 1 tsp

Instructions:

1. Clean and chop the fish into small pieces.

2. In a bowl, mix the lemon juice, chopped onion, chopped tomatoes, cilantro, jalapeno pepper, and salt.

3. Add the chopped fish to the mixture and let it marinate for 30 minutes.

4. Serve with tortilla chips or on a tostada.

TAPADO

Ingredients:

- Fish - 1 lb
- Coconut Milk - 2 cups
- Tomatoes - 2
- Onion - 1
- Garlic - 2 cloves

- Cilantro - 1/2 cup
- Plantain - 2
- Potatoes - 2
- Carrots - 2
- Corn on the cob - 2
- Chicken Broth - 2 cups
- Salt - 1 tsp

Instructions:

1. In a large pot, sauté the chopped onion and garlic in oil until translucent.

2. Add the chopped tomatoes, cilantro, and chicken broth to the pot and bring to a boil.

3. Add the fish, plantains, potatoes, carrots, and corn on the cob to the pot and let it cook for 15 minutes.

4. Pour in the coconut milk and let it simmer for an additional 5 minutes.

5. Serve hot and garnish with additional cilantro.

PESCADO AL VAPOR

Ingredients:

- Fish - 1 lb
- Lemon - 1
- Garlic - 2 cloves
- Cilantro - 1/2 cup
- Salt - 1 tsp

Instructions:

1. Clean and season the fish with lemon juice, chopped

garlic, cilantro, and salt.

2. Place the fish in a steamer basket and steam for 15-20 minutes or until fully cooked.

3. Serve hot with a side of rice and vegetables.

PESCADO EN ESCABECHE

Ingredients:

- Fish - 1 lb
- Vinegar - 1/2 cup
- Lemon Juice - 1/2 cup
- Onion - 1
- Tomatoes - 2
- Cilantro - 1/2 cup
- Jalapeno Pepper - 1
- Salt - 1 tsp

Instructions:

1. Clean and season the fish with salt and lemon juice.

2. In a separate bowl, mix the vinegar, chopped onion, chopped tomatoes, cilantro, jalapeno pepper, and salt.

3. Place the fish in a shallow dish and pour the vinegar mixture over the top.

4. Let it marinate for at least 1 hour in the refrigerator.

5. Serve as a main dish or as a side dish with rice and vegetables.

CAMARONES AL AJILLO

Ingredients:

- Shrimp - 1 lb
- Garlic - 4 cloves
- Olive Oil - 1/2 cup
- White Wine - 1/2 cup
- Lemon Juice - 1/4 cup
- Cilantro - 1/2 cup
- Salt - 1 tsp

Instructions:

1. In a pan, heat the olive oil and add the chopped garlic.

2. Add the shrimp to the pan and cook until pink, about 2-3 minutes per side.

3. Pour in the white wine and let it simmer for 1 minute.

4. Stir in the lemon juice and cilantro and season with salt.

5. Serve hot with rice or crusty bread to soak up the sauce.

SOPA DE MARISCOS

Ingredients:

- Seafood Mix (shrimp, crab, scallops, etc.) - 1 lb
- Tomatoes - 2
- Onion - 1
- Garlic - 2 cloves
- Fish Broth - 4 cups
- Cilantro - 1/2 cup

- Lemon Juice - 1/4 cup
- Potatoes - 2
- Carrots - 2
- Corn on the cob - 2
- Salt - 1 tsp

Instructions:

1. In a large pot, sauté the chopped onion and garlic in oil until translucent.

2. Add the chopped tomatoes and fish broth to the pot and bring to a boil.

3. Add the seafood mix, chopped potatoes, carrots, and corn on the cob to the pot and let it cook for 10-15 minutes.

4. Stir in the lemon juice and cilantro and season with salt.

5. Serve hot as a main dish with crusty bread to soak up the broth.

PESCADO FRITO

Ingredients:

- Fish - 1 lb
- Flour - 1 cup
- Egg - 1
- Breadcrumbs - 1 cup
- Lemon Juice - 1/4 cup
- Salt - 1 tsp
- Oil for frying

Instructions:

1. Clean and season the fish with lemon juice and salt.

2. In a shallow dish, mix the flour and salt.

3. In another shallow dish, beat the egg.

4. In a third shallow dish, place the breadcrumbs.

5. Dip each piece of fish in the flour mixture, then the egg mixture, and finally the breadcrumbs, making sure to coat well.

6. Heat the oil in a pan and fry the fish until golden brown, about 2-3 minutes per side.

7. Serve hot with lemon wedges and tartar sauce on the side.

PESCADO A LA PLANCHA

Ingredients:

- Fish - 1 lb
- Olive Oil - 1/4 cup
- Lemon Juice - 1/4 cup
- Garlic - 2 cloves
- Salt - 1 tsp

Instructions:

1. Clean and season the fish with lemon juice, chopped garlic, and salt.

2. Heat a griddle or a large pan over medium-high heat and brush with olive oil.

3. Place the fish on the griddle and cook for 3-4 minutes

per side or until fully cooked.

4. Serve hot with lemon wedges and a side of vegetables or rice.

CAMARONES A LA DIABLA

Ingredients:

- Shrimp - 1 lb
- Tomatoes - 2
- Onion - 1
- Garlic - 2 cloves
- Jalapeno Pepper - 1
- Cilantro - 1/2 cup
- Lemon Juice - 1/4 cup
- Olive Oil - 1/4 cup
- Salt - 1 tsp

Instructions:

1. In a pan, heat the olive oil and add the chopped onion, garlic, and jalapeno pepper.

2. Add the chopped tomatoes and let it cook for 2-3 minutes.

3. Add the shrimp to the pan and cook until pink, about 2-3 minutes per side.

4. Stir in the lemon juice, cilantro, and season with salt.

5. Serve hot with rice or crusty bread to soak up the sauce.

CANGREJO GUISADO

Ingredients:

- Crab - 1 lb
- Tomatoes - 2
- Onion - 1
- Garlic - 2 cloves
- Cilantro - 1/2 cup
- Lemon Juice - 1/4 cup
- Olive Oil - 1/4 cup
- Salt - 1 tsp

Instructions:

1. In a pan, heat the olive oil and add the chopped onion and garlic.

2. Add the chopped tomatoes and let it cook for 2-3 minutes.

3. Add the crab to the pan and let it cook for 5-7 minutes.

4. Stir in the lemon juice, cilantro, and season with salt.

5. Serve hot as a main dish or as a side dish with rice and vegetables.

MOJARRA EN SALSA

Ingredients:

- Fish - 1 lb
- Tomatoes - 2
- Onion - 1
- Garlic - 2 cloves
- Cilantro - 1/2 cup

- Lemon Juice - 1/4 cup
- Olive Oil - 1/4 cup
- Salt - 1 tsp
- Jalapeno Pepper - 1

Instructions:

1. In a pan, heat the olive oil and add the chopped onion, garlic, and jalapeno pepper.

2. Add the chopped tomatoes and let it cook for 2-3 minutes.

3. Add the fish to the pan and let it cook for 5-7 minutes or until fully cooked.

4. Stir in the lemon juice, cilantro, and season with salt.

5. Serve hot with rice or crusty bread to soak up the sauce.

PESCADO EN PEPIAN

Ingredients:

- Fish - 1 lb
- Tomatoes - 2
- Onion - 1
- Garlic - 2 cloves
- Cilantro - 1/2 cup
- Lemon Juice - 1/4 cup
- Olive Oil - 1/4 cup
- Salt - 1 tsp
- Pepian Sauce (made from roasted pumpkin seeds, spices, and broth) - 1 cup

Instructions:

1. In a pan, heat the olive oil and add the chopped onion and garlic.

2. Add the chopped tomatoes and let it cook for 2-3 minutes.

3. Add the fish to the pan and let it cook for 5-7 minutes or until fully cooked.

4. Stir in the lemon juice, cilantro, and season with salt.

5. Pour the pepian sauce over the top of the fish and let it simmer for 2-3 minutes.

6. Serve hot with rice or crusty bread to soak up the sauce.

PULPO EN SALSA

Ingredients:

- Octopus - 1 lb
- Tomatoes - 2
- Onion - 1
- Garlic - 2 cloves
- Cilantro - 1/2 cup
- Lemon Juice - 1/4 cup
- Olive Oil - 1/4 cup
- Salt - 1 tsp

Instructions:

1. In a pan, heat the olive oil and add the chopped onion and garlic.

2. Add the chopped tomatoes and let it cook for 2-3 minutes.

3. Add the octopus to the pan and let it cook for 8-10 minutes or until fully cooked.

4. Stir in the lemon juice, cilantro, and season with salt.

5. Serve hot with rice or crusty bread to soak up the sauce.

CAMARONES A LA CERVEZA

Ingredients:

- Shrimp - 1 lb
- Beer - 1 bottle
- Tomatoes - 2
- Onion - 1
- Garlic - 2 cloves
- Cilantro - 1/2 cup
- Lemon Juice - 1/4 cup
- Olive Oil - 1/4 cup
- Salt - 1 tsp

Instructions:

1. In a pan, heat the olive oil and add the chopped onion and garlic.

2. Add the chopped tomatoes and let it cook for 2-3 minutes.

3. Pour the beer into the pan and let it simmer for 2-3 minutes.

4. Add the shrimp to the pan and cook until pink, about 2-3 minutes per side.

5. Stir in the lemon juice, cilantro, and season with salt.

6. Serve hot with rice or crusty bread to soak up the sauce.

CALAMARES RELLENOS

Ingredients:

- Squid - 1 lb
- Stuffing (made from breadcrumbs, cheese, herbs, and spices) - 1 cup
- Egg - 1
- Flour - 1 cup
- Breadcrumbs - 1 cup
- Lemon Juice - 1/4 cup
- Salt - 1 tsp
- Oil for frying

Instructions:

1. Clean the squid and stuff each one with the stuffing mixture.

2. In a shallow dish, mix the flour and salt.

3. In another shallow dish, beat the egg.

4. In a third shallow dish, place the breadcrumbs.

5. Dip each stuffed squid in the flour mixture, then the egg mixture, and finally the breadcrumbs, making sure to coat well.

6. Heat the oil in a pan and fry the stuffed squid until golden brown, about 2-3 minutes per side.

7. Serve hot with lemon wedges and a side of vegetables or rice.

BREADS

PAN DE BANANO

Ingredients:

- Bananas - 2 ripe
- All-Purpose Flour - 2 cups
- Baking Powder - 1 tsp
- Sugar - 1/2 cup
- Eggs - 2
- Milk - 1/2 cup
- Vanilla Extract - 1 tsp
- Salt - 1/4 tsp

Instructions:

1. Preheat oven to 350°F (180°C).

2. In a bowl, mash the ripe bananas with a fork until smooth.

3. In another bowl, mix together the flour, baking powder, and salt.

4. In a large bowl, beat together the eggs, sugar, milk, and vanilla extract until well combined.

5. Gradually add the dry ingredients to the wet mixture and mix until just combined.

6. Fold in the mashed bananas until evenly distributed.

7. Pour the batter into a greased 9x5 inch (23x13 cm) loaf pan and bake for 40-45 minutes, or until a toothpick

inserted into the center comes out clean.

8. Allow the bread to cool for 10 minutes in the pan, then transfer to a wire rack to cool completely.

PAN DE YEMA

Ingredients:

- All-Purpose Flour - 2 cups
- Baking Powder - 1 tsp
- Sugar - 1 cup
- Eggs - 4
- Yolks - 8
- Milk - 1 cup
- Vanilla Extract - 1 tsp
- Salt - 1/4 tsp
- Lemon Zest - 1 tsp
- Butter - 1/2 cup

Instructions:

1. Preheat oven to 350°F (180°C).

2. In a bowl, mix together the flour, baking powder, and salt.

3. In a separate bowl, beat the eggs and egg yolks together until light and frothy.

4. In a saucepan, heat the milk, sugar, lemon zest, and butter over medium heat until the butter is melted and the sugar is dissolved.

5. Gradually add the dry ingredients to the egg mixture, then add the warm milk mixture, and mix until just combined.

6. Pour the batter into a greased 9x5 inch (23x13 cm) loaf pan and bake for 40-45 minutes, or until a toothpick inserted into the center comes out clean.

7. Allow the bread to cool for 10 minutes in the pan, then transfer to a wire rack to cool completely.

CHAPATA CHAPINA

Ingredients:

- All-Purpose Flour - 2 cups
- Instant Yeast - 1 tsp
- Salt - 1 tsp
- Sugar - 1 tsp
- Warm Water - 1 cup
- Olive Oil - 2 tbsp

Instructions:

1. In a large bowl, mix together the flour, yeast, salt, and sugar.

2. Gradually add the warm water and olive oil, mixing with a spoon until a dough forms.

3. Turn the dough out onto a floured surface and knead for 10 minutes, or until smooth and elastic.

4. Place the dough in a greased bowl, cover with plastic wrap, and let rise in a warm place for 1 hour, or until doubled in size.

5. Preheat oven to 400°F (200°C).

6. Divide the dough into 8 equal pieces and shape into rounds.

7. Place the rounds on a baking sheet and bake for 15-20 minutes, or until golden brown.

8. Serve hot or at room temperature.

TORTA DE ELOTE

Ingredients:

- Corn Flour - 2 cups
- All-Purpose Flour - 1 cup
- Baking Powder - 1 tbsp
- Salt - 1 tsp
- Sugar - 1/2 cup
- Eggs - 2
- Milk - 1 cup
- Corn Kernels - 1 cup
- Cotija Cheese - 1 cup
- Jalapeno Peppers - 2, diced
- Cilantro - 1/4 cup, chopped

Instructions:

1. Preheat oven to 350°F (180°C).

2. In a large bowl, mix together the corn flour, all-purpose flour, baking powder, and salt.

3. In another bowl, beat together the eggs, sugar, and milk.

4. Gradually add the dry ingredients to the wet mixture, mixing until just combined.

5. Fold in the corn kernels, cotija cheese, jalapeno peppers, and cilantro until evenly distributed.

6. Pour the batter into a greased 9-inch (23 cm) round cake pan.

7. Bake for 30-35 minutes, or until a toothpick inserted into the center comes out clean.

8. Allow the torta to cool for 10 minutes in the pan, then transfer to a wire rack to cool completely.

PAN DE QUESO

Ingredients:

- All-Purpose Flour - 2 cups
- Baking Powder - 1 tsp
- Salt - 1/4 tsp
- Sugar - 1/2 cup
- Eggs - 2
- Milk - 1/2 cup
- Queso Fresco - 1 cup, crumbled
- Vanilla Extract - 1 tsp

Instructions:

1. Preheat oven to 350°F (180°C).

2. In a bowl, mix together the flour, baking powder, and salt.

3. In another bowl, beat together the eggs, sugar, milk, and vanilla extract until well combined.

4. Gradually add the dry ingredients to the wet mixture and mix until just combined.

5. Fold in the crumbled queso fresco until evenly distributed.

6. Pour the batter into a greased 9x5 inch (23x13 cm) loaf pan and bake for 40-45 minutes, or until a toothpick inserted into the center comes out clean.

7. Allow the bread to cool for 10 minutes in the pan, then transfer to a wire rack to cool completely.

ROSQUILLAS

Ingredients:

- All-Purpose Flour - 2 cups
- Baking Powder - 1 tsp
- Salt - 1/4 tsp
- Sugar - 1 cup
- Eggs - 2
- Milk - 1/2 cup
- Vanilla Extract - 1 tsp
- Cinnamon - 1 tsp
- Vegetable Oil - for frying

Instructions:

1. In a bowl, mix together the flour, baking powder, and salt.

2. In another bowl, beat together the eggs, sugar, milk, and vanilla extract until well combined.

3. Gradually add the dry ingredients to the wet mixture and mix until just combined.

4. In a small bowl, mix together the sugar and cinnamon for coating the rosquillas.

5. Heat the vegetable oil in a large, deep saucepan over medium heat until hot.

6. Using a cookie scoop or a tablespoon, drop rounded spoonfuls of the batter into the hot oil and cook until golden brown, about 2-3 minutes per side.

7. Using a slotted spoon, remove the rosquillas from the oil and drain on paper towels.

8. Roll the rosquillas in the cinnamon sugar mixture while still warm.

9. Serve warm or at room temperature.

MOLLETES

Ingredients:

- Bolillo Rolls - 4
- Refried Beans - 1 cup
- Queso Fresco - 1 cup, crumbled
- Jalapeno Peppers - 2, diced

Instructions:

1. Preheat oven to 375°F (190°C).

2. Cut the bolillo rolls in half horizontally and spread refried beans on the cut sides of the rolls.

3. Sprinkle crumbled queso fresco and diced jalapeno peppers on top of the refried beans.

4. Place the molletes on a baking sheet and bake for 10-15 minutes, or until the cheese is melted and bubbly.

5. Serve warm.

SEMITAS

Ingredients:

- All-Purpose Flour - 2 cups
- Instant Yeast - 1 tsp
- Salt - 1 tsp
- Sugar - 1 tsp
- Warm Water - 1 cup
- Anise Seeds - 1 tsp
- Vegetable Oil - for frying

Instructions:

1. In a large bowl, mix together the flour, yeast, salt, sugar, and anise seeds.

2. Gradually add the warm water, mixing with a spoon until a dough forms.

3. Turn the dough out onto a floured surface and knead for 10 minutes, or until smooth and elastic.

4. Place the dough in a greased bowl, cover with plastic wrap, and let rise in a warm place for 1 hour, or until doubled in size.

5. Heat the vegetable oil in a large, deep saucepan over medium heat until hot.

6. Divide the dough into 8 equal pieces and shape into rounds.

7. Fry the rounds in the hot oil until golden brown, about 2-3 minutes per side.

8. Drain the semitas on paper towels and sprinkle with

sugar while still warm.

9. Serve warm or at room temperature.

TORREJAS

Ingredients:

- Brioche Bread - 4 slices
- Milk - 1 cup
- Cinnamon - 1 tsp
- Sugar - 1/2 cup
- Eggs - 2
- Vanilla Extract - 1 tsp
- Vegetable Oil - for frying
- Powdered Sugar - for dusting

Instructions:

1. Cut the brioche bread into 2-inch (5 cm) thick slices.

2. In a shallow bowl, mix together the milk, cinnamon, and sugar.

3. In another shallow bowl, beat together the eggs and vanilla extract.

4. Dip each slice of bread in the milk mixture, then in the egg mixture, making sure both sides are well coated.

5. Heat the vegetable oil in a large, deep saucepan over medium heat until hot.

6. Fry the slices of bread in the hot oil until golden brown, about 2-3 minutes per side.

7. Drain the torrejas on paper towels and sprinkle with

powdered sugar while still warm.

8. Serve warm or at room temperature.

SHUCAS

Ingredients:

- Maize Flour - 2 cups
- Water - 1 1/2 cups
- Salt - 1 tsp
- Vegetable Oil - for frying

Instructions:

1. In a large bowl, mix together the maize flour, water, and salt until a dough forms.

2. Divide the dough into 8 equal pieces and shape into rounds.

3. Heat the vegetable oil in a large, deep saucepan over medium heat until hot.

4. Fry the rounds in the hot oil until golden brown, about 2-3 minutes per side.

5. Drain the shucas on paper towels and sprinkle with salt while still warm.

6. Serve warm or at room temperature.

SHECAS

Ingredients:

- Maize Flour - 2 cups

- Water - 1 1/2 cups
- Salt - 1 tsp
- Sugar - 1/4 cup
- Vegetable Oil - for frying

Instructions:

1. In a large bowl, mix together the maize flour, water, and salt until a dough forms.

2. Divide the dough into 8 equal pieces and shape into rounds.

3. Heat the vegetable oil in a large, deep saucepan over medium heat until hot.

4. Fry the rounds in the hot oil until golden brown, about 2-3 minutes per side.

5. Drain the shecas on paper towels and sprinkle with sugar while still warm.

6. Serve warm or at room temperature.

PAN DE LECHE

Ingredients:

- All-Purpose Flour - 2 cups
- Baking Powder - 1 tsp
- Salt - 1/4 tsp
- Sugar - 1 cup
- Eggs - 2
- Milk - 1 cup
- Vanilla Extract - 1 tsp
- Unsalted Butter - 1/2 cup, melted

Instructions:

1. Preheat oven to 350°F (180°C).

2. In a bowl, mix together the flour, baking powder, and salt.

3. In another bowl, beat together the eggs, sugar, milk, vanilla extract, and melted butter until well combined.

4. Gradually add the dry ingredients to the wet mixture and mix until just combined.

5. Pour the batter into a greased 9x5 inch (23x13 cm) loaf pan and bake for 40-45 minutes, or until a toothpick inserted into the center comes out clean.

6. Allow the bread to cool for 10 minutes in the pan, then transfer to a wire rack to cool completely.

PAN DE COCO

Ingredients:

- All-Purpose Flour - 2 cups
- Baking Powder - 1 tsp
- Salt - 1/4 tsp
- Sugar - 1/2 cup
- Eggs - 2
- Milk - 1/2 cup
- Shredded Coconut - 1 cup
- Vanilla Extract - 1 tsp

Instructions:

1. Preheat oven to 350°F (180°C).

2. In a bowl, mix together the flour, baking powder, and salt.

3. In another bowl, beat together the eggs, sugar, milk, and vanilla extract until well combined.

4. Gradually add the dry ingredients to the wet mixture and mix until just combined.

5. Stir in the shredded coconut.

6. Pour the batter into a greased 9x5 inch (23x13 cm) loaf pan and bake for 40-45 minutes, or until a toothpick inserted into the center comes out clean.

7. Allow the bread to cool for 10 minutes in the pan, then transfer to a wire rack to cool completely.

PAN DE AYOTE

Ingredients:

- All-Purpose Flour - 2 cups
- Baking Powder - 1 tsp
- Salt - 1/4 tsp
- Sugar - 1/2 cup
- Eggs - 2
- Milk - 1/2 cup
- Mashed Ayote - 1 cup
- Vanilla Extract - 1 tsp

Instructions:

1. Preheat oven to 350°F (180°C).

2. In a bowl, mix together the flour, baking powder, and salt.

3. In another bowl, beat together the eggs, sugar, milk, and vanilla extract until well combined.

4. Gradually add the dry ingredients to the wet mixture and mix until just combined.

5. Stir in the mashed ayote.

6. Pour the batter into a greased 9x5 inch (23x13 cm) loaf pan and bake for 40-45 minutes, or until a toothpick inserted into the center comes out clean.

7. Allow the bread to cool for 10 minutes in the pan, then transfer to a wire rack to cool completely.

PAN DULCE

Ingredients:

- All-Purpose Flour - 2 cups
- Baking Powder - 1 tsp
- Salt - 1/4 tsp
- Sugar - 1 cup
- Eggs - 2
- Milk - 1/2 cup
- Vanilla Extract - 1 tsp
- Unsalted Butter - 1/2 cup, melted
- Sprinkles - for decoration

Instructions:

1. Preheat oven to 350°F (180°C).

2. In a bowl, mix together the flour, baking powder, and salt.

3. In another bowl, beat together the eggs, sugar, milk,

vanilla extract, and melted butter until well combined.

4. Gradually add the dry ingredients to the wet mixture and mix until just combined.

5. Pour the batter into a greased 9x5 inch (23x13 cm) loaf pan and sprinkle the top with sprinkles.

6. Bake for 40-45 minutes, or until a toothpick inserted into the center comes out clean.

7. Allow the bread to cool for 10 minutes in the pan, then transfer to a wire rack to cool completely.

DESSERTS

BUÑUELOS

Ingredients:

- Flour - 2 cups
- Baking Powder - 2 teaspoons
- Eggs - 2
- Water - 1 cup
- Salt - 1/2 teaspoon
- Vegetable Oil - for frying

Instructions:

1. In a large bowl, mix together the flour, baking powder, and salt.

2. Beat the eggs in a separate bowl and add to the dry ingredients, along with the water. Mix until well combined.

3. Heat the oil in a large frying pan over medium-high heat.

4. Using a spoon or cookie scoop, drop spoonfuls of the batter into the hot oil and fry until golden brown, about 2 minutes per side.

5. Remove the buñuelos from the oil with a slotted spoon and drain on paper towels.

6. Serve warm with a sprinkle of cinnamon sugar or a drizzle of honey, if desired.

RELLENITOS DE PLÁTANO

Ingredients:

- Ripe Plantains - 2
- Black Beans - 1 cup
- Cinnamon - 1 teaspoon
- Sugar - 1/4 cup
- Vegetable Oil - for frying

Instructions:

1. Peel and mash the plantains in a large bowl.

2. In a separate bowl, mix together the black beans, cinnamon, and sugar.

3. Using your hands, form the mashed plantains into small balls and make an indentation in the center. Fill the indentation with a spoonful of the black bean mixture.

4. Heat the oil in a large frying pan over medium-high heat.

5. Fry the rellenitos in the hot oil until golden brown, about 2 minutes per side.

6. Remove from the oil with a slotted spoon and drain on paper towels.

7. Serve warm as a sweet snack or dessert.

CANILLITAS DE LECHE

Ingredients:

- Milk - 2 cups
- Cinnamon Sticks - 2
- Lemon Peel - 1
- Sugar - 1/2 cup
- Cornstarch - 2 tablespoons
- Eggs - 2
- Vanilla Extract - 1 teaspoon
- Ground Cinnamon - 1/2 teaspoon
- Powdered Sugar - for dusting

Instructions:

1. In a medium saucepan, combine the milk, cinnamon sticks, lemon peel, and sugar. Heat over medium heat until the sugar has dissolved.

2. In a small bowl, whisk together the cornstarch, eggs, and vanilla extract.

3. Gradually add the egg mixture to the milk mixture, stirring constantly, until the mixture thickens, about 5 minutes.

4. Remove from heat and let cool.

5. Once cooled, remove the cinnamon sticks and lemon peel.

6. Pour the mixture into individual cups or a large serving dish.

7. Sprinkle with ground cinnamon and dust with powdered sugar before serving.

TRES LECHES

Ingredients:

- All-Purpose Flour - 1 1/2 cups
- Baking Powder - 1 tablespoon
- Salt - 1/4 teaspoon
- Eggs - 6
- Sugar - 1 cup
- Vanilla Extract - 1 teaspoon
- Milk - 1 can (14 oz) of condensed milk
- Heavy Cream - 1 can (12 oz) of evaporated milk
- Whole Milk - 1 cup
- Powdered Sugar - for dusting

Instructions:

1. Preheat the oven to 350°F (175°C). Grease a 9x13 inch baking dish.

2. In a medium bowl, whisk together the flour, baking powder, and salt. Set aside.

3. In a large bowl, beat the eggs until light and frothy. Gradually add the sugar and beat until thick and lemon-colored. Stir in the vanilla extract.

4. Gradually add the flour mixture to the egg mixture and mix until well combined. Pour the batter into the prepared baking dish.

5. Bake for 30-35 minutes, or until a toothpick inserted into the center of the cake comes out clean.

6. While the cake is baking, combine the condensed milk, evaporated milk, and whole milk in a large bowl.

7. Once the cake is done, remove from the oven and let cool for 10 minutes. Using a fork, poke holes all over the top of the cake.

8. Gradually pour the milk mixture over the cake, allowing it to soak in. Let the cake cool completely.

9. Once cooled, spread whipped cream over the top of the cake and sprinkle with powdered sugar before serving.

FLAN CHAPIN

Ingredients:

- Sugar - 1 cup
- Water - 1/4 cup
- Sweetened Condensed Milk - 1 can (14 oz)
- Evaporated Milk - 1 can (12 oz)
- Eggs - 6
- Vanilla Extract - 1 teaspoon
- Cinnamon - 1/2 teaspoon

Instructions:

1. Preheat the oven to 350°F (175°C). Grease a 9-inch round cake pan.

2. In a small saucepan, combine the sugar and water. Heat over medium heat until the sugar has dissolved and the mixture has turned golden brown, about 5 minutes. Pour the caramel into the prepared cake pan, swirling to coat the bottom.

3. In a large bowl, whisk together the condensed milk, evaporated milk, eggs, vanilla extract, and cinnamon. Pour the mixture over the caramel in the cake pan.

4. Place the cake pan in a larger baking dish and fill the larger dish with hot water to create a water bath.

5. Bake for 50-60 minutes, or until the flan is set and no longer jiggles.

6. Remove from the oven and let cool to room temperature. Once cooled, refrigerate for at least 2 hours, or overnight.

7. To serve, run a knife around the edge of the flan and invert onto a serving dish. The caramel should be on top. Serve chilled.

PASTEL DE ELOTE

Ingredients:

- Corn - 3 cups
- Sugar - 1/2 cup
- Eggs - 4
- Heavy Cream - 1/2 cup
- All-Purpose Flour - 1/2 cup
- Baking Powder - 1 teaspoon
- Salt - 1/4 teaspoon
- Vanilla Extract - 1 teaspoon

Instructions:

1. Preheat the oven to 350°F (175°C). Grease a 9-inch round cake pan.

2. In a large bowl, mix together the corn, sugar, eggs, heavy cream, flour, baking powder, salt, and vanilla extract. Pour the mixture into the prepared cake pan.

3. Bake for 35-40 minutes, or until a toothpick inserted

into the center of the cake comes out clean.

4. Remove from the oven and let cool to room temperature. Serve as a sweet snack or dessert.

ARROZ EN LECHE

Ingredients:

- Rice - 1 cup
- Milk - 4 cups
- Cinnamon Sticks - 2
- Lemon Peel - 1
- Sugar - 1/2 cup
- Vanilla Extract - 1 teaspoon
- Raisins - 1/2 cup (optional)

Instructions:

1. In a medium saucepan, combine the rice, milk, cinnamon sticks, lemon peel, and sugar. Heat over medium heat until the mixture comes to a boil.

2. Reduce heat to low and let simmer, stirring occasionally, until the rice is tender and the mixture has thickened, about 20-25 minutes.

3. Remove from heat and stir in the vanilla extract and raisins (if using). Let cool to room temperature.

4. Once cooled, remove the cinnamon sticks and lemon peel. Serve as a warm sweet pudding.

EMPANADAS DE LECHE

Ingredients:

- All-Purpose Flour - 2 cups
- Baking Powder - 1 teaspoon
- Salt - 1/4 teaspoon
- Shortening - 1/2 cup
- Water - 1/4 cup
- Milk - 2 cups
- Sugar - 1/2 cup
- Lemon Peel - 1
- Cinnamon Sticks - 2
- Eggs - 2
- Vanilla Extract - 1 teaspoon
- Ground Cinnamon - 1 teaspoon

Instructions:

1. In a medium bowl, whisk together the flour, baking powder, and salt. Cut in the shortening until the mixture resembles coarse crumbs. Gradually add the water and mix until a dough forms.

2. Roll out the dough on a lightly floured surface to 1/8 inch thickness. Cut into 4-inch circles.

3. In a medium saucepan, combine the milk, sugar, lemon peel, and cinnamon sticks. Heat over medium heat until the sugar has dissolved.

4. In a small bowl, beat together the eggs and vanilla extract. Gradually add the egg mixture to the milk mixture, stirring constantly, until the mixture thickens, about 5 minutes. Remove from heat and let cool to room temperature.

5. Once the filling has cooled, remove the cinnamon sticks and lemon peel. Spoon 1-2 tablespoons of the filling onto one half of each dough circle. Fold the dough over to create a half-moon shape and press the edges together to seal.

6. Heat a large skillet over medium heat. Cook the empanadas until they are golden brown on both sides, about 2-3 minutes per side.

7. Remove from heat and let cool for a few minutes. Serve warm, sprinkled with ground cinnamon.

CHOCO BANANO

Ingredients:

- Bananas - 4
- Chocolate Chips - 1 cup
- Shortening - 2 tablespoons
- Ground Cinnamon - 1/2 teaspoon

Instructions:

1. Peel the bananas and cut them in half crosswise.

2. In a small saucepan, combine the chocolate chips and shortening. Heat over low heat, stirring constantly, until the chocolate is melted and smooth.

3. Dip each banana half into the melted chocolate, making sure to coat it completely. Place the coated bananas on a parchment-lined baking sheet.

4. Sprinkle the ground cinnamon over the chocolate-coated bananas.

5. Place the baking sheet in the freezer for 30 minutes, or until the chocolate has hardened.

6. Remove from the freezer and serve as a sweet, frozen treat.

NUEGADOS

Ingredients:

- Yellow Corn Masa - 2 cups
- Water - 1/2 cup
- Lard or Vegetable Shortening - 1/2 cup
- Ground Cinnamon - 1 teaspoon
- Sugar - 1/2 cup
- Oil - for frying

Instructions:

1. In a large bowl, mix together the corn masa, water, lard or shortening, cinnamon, and sugar. The mixture should be smooth and pliable.

2. Heat the oil in a large saucepan over medium heat.

3. Using your hands, shape the masa mixture into small balls, about the size of a golf ball.

4. Carefully drop the balls into the hot oil and fry until they are golden brown on all sides, about 3-5 minutes.

5. Remove from heat and drain on a paper towel-lined plate.

6. Once cooled, roll the nuegados in additional sugar before serving.

MAZAPANES

Ingredients:

- Peanuts - 1 1/2 cups
- Powdered Sugar - 1 1/2 cups
- Almond Meal - 1/2 cup
- Vanilla Extract - 1 teaspoon
- Honey - 2 tablespoons

Instructions:

1. Preheat the oven to 350°F (175°C). Line a baking sheet with parchment paper.

2. In a food processor, pulse the peanuts until they are finely ground.

3. In a large bowl, mix together the ground peanuts, powdered sugar, almond meal, vanilla extract, and honey. The mixture should be crumbly but able to hold its shape when molded.

4. Roll the mixture into 1-inch balls and place them on the prepared baking sheet.

5. Bake for 10-12 minutes, or until the mazapanes are lightly golden.

6. Remove from the oven and let cool to room temperature. Serve as a sweet snack or dessert.

MARQUESOTE

Ingredients:

- All-Purpose Flour - 2 cups

- Baking Powder - 2 teaspoons
- Eggs - 4
- Sugar - 1 cup
- Milk - 1 cup
- Vanilla Extract - 1 teaspoon
- Cinnamon - 1 teaspoon
- Cloves - 1/4 teaspoon

Instructions:

1. Preheat the oven to 350°F (175°C). Grease a 9-inch round cake pan.

2. In a medium bowl, whisk together the flour and baking powder.

3. In a large bowl, beat together the eggs and sugar until light and fluffy. Gradually add the milk, vanilla extract, cinnamon, and cloves, beating until well combined.

4. Gradually add the flour mixture to the egg mixture, mixing until just combined. Pour the batter into the prepared cake pan.

5. Bake for 35-40 minutes, or until a toothpick inserted into the center of the cake comes out clean.

6. Remove from the oven and let cool to room temperature. Serve as a sweet snack or dessert.

COCADAS

Ingredients:

- Coconut Milk - 1 can (14 oz)
- Sugar - 1 cup
- Egg Whites - 2

- Vanilla Extract - 1 teaspoon
- Shredded Coconut - 1 cup

Instructions:

1. Preheat the oven to 325°F (165°C). Line a baking sheet with parchment paper.

2. In a medium saucepan, combine the coconut milk and sugar. Heat over medium heat, stirring constantly, until the sugar has dissolved.

3. In a large bowl, beat the egg whites until stiff peaks form. Gradually add the hot coconut milk mixture to the egg whites, beating constantly. Stir in the vanilla extract.

4. Fold in the shredded coconut.

5. Drop the mixture by spoonfuls onto the prepared baking sheet. Bake for 20-25 minutes, or until the cocadas are lightly golden.

6. Remove from the oven and let cool to room temperature. Serve as a sweet snack or dessert.

GALLETAS DE AJEDREZ

Ingredients:

- All-Purpose Flour - 2 1/2 cups
- Baking Powder - 1 teaspoon
- Salt - 1/4 teaspoon
- Unsalted Butter - 1 cup (softened)
- Sugar - 1 cup
- Eggs - 2
- Vanilla Extract - 1 teaspoon
- Unsweetened Cocoa Powder - 1/2 cup

Instructions:

1. Preheat the oven to 375°F (190°C). Line a baking sheet with parchment paper.

2. In a medium bowl, whisk together the flour, baking powder, and salt.

3. In a large bowl, beat together the butter and sugar until light and fluffy. Beat in the eggs one at a time, then stir in the vanilla extract.

4. Gradually add the flour mixture to the butter mixture, mixing until just combined. Divide the dough in half.

5. In one half of the dough, stir in the cocoa powder until well combined.

6. Using a cookie scoop or spoon, drop alternating spoonfuls of the vanilla and chocolate dough onto the prepared baking sheet, creating a checkerboard pattern. Using a toothpick, swirl the dough together lightly to create a marbled effect.

7. Bake for 10-12 minutes, or until the cookies are lightly golden.

8. Remove from the oven and let cool on the baking sheet for 5 minutes before transferring to a wire rack to cool completely. Serve as a sweet snack or dessert.

RECIPES LIST

APPETIZERS

SOUPS

SALADS

VEGETABLES

SIDE DISHES

PORK

BEEF

CHICKEN

SEAFOOD

BREADS

DESSERTS

Printed in Great Britain
by Amazon